MW00626523

An Intimate Look at Wine

Michael Charles Lapmardo
MC Productions
8720 East Market
Warren, OH 44484
(330) 856-9463

ISBN 0-9651849-0-0

50999

9 780965 184908

*Dedicated to people everywhere
who make, drink, and cherish wine—
may your cup runneth over!*

TABLE OF CONTENTS

INTRODUCTION

Wine, First Impressions

PRONUNCIATION GUIDE
INTRODUCTION

Connoisseur (kah nah soo´ er)
a person who likes to drink wine, and talk about it to others.

Barnyard (barn yard)
A taste associated with some Italian wines and good red wines. When present and in a balanced wine, it will add earthy complexity to the fruit by suggesting hints of fresh country air during fertilization time.

Tartaric acid (tar tar´ ik)
the acid that is present in wine from the grapes.

INTRODUCTION

Wine, First Impressions

Probably one of the most difficult aspects of appreciating and enjoying wine, is learning how to taste it, and what to expect once the wine is out of the bottle and in your mouth. When tasting with friends, or helping someone pick a bottle of wine for dinner, they will at some point usually say "I'm not a connoisseur." My general reply is "you don't have to be a connoisseur, you just have to like wine, and have an opinion."

What is a connoisseur? It is someone who likes wine, and has something definite to say about it. We often think of the connoisseur as a storehouse of knowledge, a traveler of strange and foreign lands who has consumed wine on all the continents, and speaks English with the hint of some foreign accent still lingering. But you and I are connoisseurs. You don't have to be an expert to enjoy wine, you just have to drink it.

This is the one, undeniable, absolute, and unqualified aspect of enjoying wine. Drinking wine is like learning a new language. At first everything is unfamiliar and there seems to be no real distinction between similar red wines—or similar words. Wine tastes are enormously helpful— as is traveling to a country where the language is being spoken—and our continual exposure to the phraseology and nuances of meaning, little by little begin to sink in. We grasp a word here—a flavor that we tasted in another wine is also present in this one—what is that? What is he saying— I want to learn more! And so we learn, little by little and step by step.

The most difficult part of learning a language or learning about what to look for when tasting wine is the unfamiliarity with the new subject. We have nothing with which to compare our new experiences. What is wine supposed to taste like? What are we to expect? To look for?

A lot of times, we can try to educate ourselves on the subject before actually getting into it. In this way, you can make the relationship between what is known, and apply it to the unknown.

For example, I remember while a Freshman in college placing what I thought was a banana covered with heavy whip cream on my tray one day while going through the food line. I couldn't wait to dig into that delicious dessert. I picked up a forkful of the banana and covered it with the rich and creamy topping, placing it in my mouth I expected to be titillated with fantastic sensations of sweet cream and soft ripe banana, instead, and with great horror, I spit the whole noxious mouthful back into my dish! It wasn't cream at all; it was mayonnaise!

Whoever heard of putting mayonnaise on a banana! I was speechless. Now, if someone had told me that this was a banana covered with mayo, I would have gotten ready for a new taste sensation—one that I might question—but nevertheless, prepared myself for. Like putting raisins in salad, you would like to know they are in there, so when you bite down on something squishy, you're not wandering whether to swallow or spit out the mouthful. But I think of this story every time I introduce somebody new to wine. A lot of people have never tasted wine, and if you give someone a glass of dry red Cabernet without the proper introductions and explanations, they might have a look on their face after the first sip as that of someone trying to stifle a burp of a hot dog he ate three days ago.

You have to be prepared for these new concepts, either by educating yourself through tasting and reading, or by being around people who enjoy wine so you can look for the new experiences while being guided by a knowledgeable person who can bring you from the unfamiliar to the familiar.

What we will try to do in the following pages is bring you from the unknown to the known. From how you experience wine for the first time, to an experienced taster of note and notoriety.

First of all, a wine is 100% fruit, so you can expect some of the flavors you may associate with fruit. A white wine may have subtle flavors of pineapple, mangos, and tropical fruit. (I remember saying this one time and a gentleman said "do they actually put that stuff in there?")

I just said that since wine is fruit, and the roots of the grape vine are very extensive, it may pick up subtle nuances of flavors from surrounding plants and even trees.

Joe Heitz of Heitz Vineyards of California bottles a special wine he calls Heitz "Martha's vineyard" in which the taste of eucalyptus is very noticeable, and this, Joe says, is from the row of eucalyptus trees bordering the area of grapes he uses to make the Martha's Vineyard.

The grapes themselves, depending on the variety, may have unique flavors. For example Sauvignon Blanc is very herbaceous and grassy. It actually smells like fresh cut grass at times, but if you give someone a glass of Sauvignon Blanc without at least suggesting herbs and fresh cut grass, they may think that this dry white wine is just sharp and acidic, or has some "off" taste that they can't describe. But suggesting fresh cut grass and herbs not only puts kind of a positive spin on the wine, it gives the person a point of reference he can draw from his storehouse of flavor concepts and known entities, so he can apply it to something he is tasting for the first time and have some idea of either what the wine is reminiscent of, or the sensation that is registering in his mouth.

For this reason, tasting wine in a group with each person describing what he or she feels about the wine is a very important way to learn about wine. Make sure there are some wine experts in the group, and people who are conversant with the language of wine. You'll pick these terms and descriptions up quickly.

A friend of ours is a high school chemistry teacher, and an avid wine drinker. We were tasting some Gamay wine one day, and he said that a certain bottle had "geranial spoilage." "What is that?" I howled, mostly laughing, for this man had a penchant for scientific terms applied to wine which absolutely no one had heard of.

> **CONSUMER TIP**
>
> Try adding more whole foods and natural products to your diet. Cut out the use of sugars and sweeteners and learn how to enjoy food in their natural state. You'll discover that after a while, you will no longer crave fats and sugars; you will have reprogrammed your palate!
>
> This is not only beneficial as far as enjoying foods is concerned, but also much more healthy. You will lose weight, look and feel better, and have a better opinion about yourself. Wine is a natural product that fits well into this type of lifestyle.
>
> Once you start feeling better, you will have the energy and stamina to do many more things, and you'll find that your whole outlook on life will have changed.

He just said "have you ever smelled a spoiled or rotten geranium?" Being an avid gardener, I thought hard, and in the many wonderful sights and smells that I had registered in the last 43 years—most of which spent growing things—I could not ever recall the scent of a rotting geranium. It's almost impossible to kill a geranium. You can pull them out of the ground and let the sun beat on the roots and leaves for weeks, and they look O.K. You can put them on a compost heap, and two years later they will still have flowers—they are almost impossible to destroy! Geraniual spoilage? Ah well.

But this same gentleman brought me to the love of Italian wines when we were tasting Italians one night early in my experience as a wine lover. We opened an old Brunello, and upon tasting it I immediately thought that this bottle had been horribly spoiled—it tasted like, honest to God, this is exactly what I thought, hay and horse crap mixed together.

I looked at some of the other faces around the table, and I thought "could anybody possible be thinking the same thing that I am?" They couldn't possibly be thinking hay and horse crap. I tasted again. Hay and horse crap.

One by one we went around the table relating our impressions of the wine. People were gushing adjectives like "tobacco-ey" and "chocolately" and "coffee-like" or "tar-like", but no one mentioned horse shit! Until it was my turn. I have many imperfections, but holding in what I feel has never been one of them—especially after about 6 glasses of wine.

"This tastes like hay and horse crap" I exclaimed. And without even batting an eyelash, our chemistry teacher friend calmly said "Classic Barn-yard of an old Italian—fantastic isn't it." I was stunned. Many of the first time wine drinkers looked up to me and anxiously awaited my comments after that episode, and it was one that I think of most—along with the mayo-covered banana, when I listen to someone with great enthusiasm trying to discern the great rush of new flavors that are attacking his mouth, with absolutely no point of reference with which he can describe these great new sensations. Just say what you feel and what you taste. Other people might be thinking the same thing.

We are going to talk about some of the flavors you would taste in some of the grape varieties next. Hopefully these flavor concepts will en-able you to make the connection to something known and pleasant when you put that first sip of wine into your mouth. They will also give you a working vocabulary with which to converse about wine to others.

White wines can taste like: flowers, fruit, spice, grass, vegetables and herbs, minerals. Red wines can have tastes of berries, vegetables, toast, earth, coffee, mocha, tobacco, chocolate, earth, and tar.

On first tasting wines, you will not be able to discern a lot of flavors, but understanding that there are subtle flavors like the ones described above in wine will allow you to be aware of these concepts, and they will then start to emerge as you become a more experienced taster.

At the very least, even if the wines you are tasting don't have nuances of the flavors you are describing or experiencing, they at least give you a point of reference as to the flavor concept of the wine, and, after all, you are the one who will eventually decide whether you like the wine or not.

In addition to flavor nuances described above, wine will be dry, or sweet, or bitter, and also have textures like full and fleshy, or lean and thin. Wine tastes different at different temperatures, and from different glasses, so there is a lot to be considered when taking that first sip of wine and trying to make the connection from what is known to what is unknown.

Most people like sweets, or the taste of sugar. Fresh ripe fruit is often very sweet, and there is no denying the love we all have for our favorite candy. Vegetables on the other hand are not usually sweet, and it takes a more mature palate to enjoy the rich earthy flavor of brussels sprouts, or broccoli and kale, and some of the other garden delectables.

So it is with wine. While we all like the sweet, the sugar in most red wines is fermented into alcohol. Alcohol gives wine its structure, or the backbone on which the wine is to be built. The acid from the grapes, tartaric acid, is another element on which good wine is built. The acid can be compared to the musculature.

Indeed, a wine with little acid just kind of lays in your mouth kind of "fat and lazy" and we call these wines "flabby or fat." The taste of fruit is like the skin; seductive and beautiful, it calls to us with its hedonistic flavors. The presence of the wine in our mouth will at once provide many impressions. The bitter or puckery taste of the tannins will be felt at the back of our tongue; this is where we register bitterness. The sides of our tongue will register the acid—what we may construe as sour, and in the front of our tongue, we will taste the sweetness of the wine.

In addition to this, since wine is volatile—especially red wine—it will etherize and the aromas will drift into our sinuses up the back of our throats. Here we will experience the wine through our olfactory senses.

We are able to discern many more flavors and nuances of flavor here. As our brain assimilates all the data rushing in, calling from known store-houses of billions of bits of data and tasting experience, we will form opinions about wines, and the more familiar we are with a certain flavor, the more comfortable it is to us, and the more understanding we are of it; we simply get used to the flavor. For example, Heinz ketchup. Everybody loves Heinz Ketchup—what's not to like? Tomatoes, sugar, nice texture, but we have learned to like it because we are so familiar with it. The advertisers made us feel at home with it, and before long, whether it tasted like real tomatoes or not, we were used to the taste of Heinz Ketchup.

Just like real maple syrup. Sounds delicious. But most of us are used to the 97% sugar and imitation maple flavor in our syrups and because we are used to it, would probably have to reacquaint ourselves with what real maple syrup tastes like. Once we get used to the taste of wine, the dryness, the tannin, the alcohol, we are familiar with it, and from that point can start to differentiate among the plethora of flavors it presents us with.

If a wine is fruity, we may expect to taste a bit of sweetness, and when we don't we may bring up past memories of a sour or tart or unripe piece of fruit. This is a negative connotation and if the connection is made this way, we will not like wine.

Take my dad. He puts sugar on everything—frosted flakes, cantaloupe, strawberries, you name it, he puts sugar on it. Give him a glass of good Cabernet and guess what; he takes a sip, looks at me dolefully and smacks his lips and shakes his head; "too dry" he exclaims. "Well your mouth is coated with sugar for God's sake!" But he, like millions of other people, is used to the taste of sweets.

Wine is fruity, with subtle nuances and hints of blackberries and blueberries and earth. This doesn't mean it's going to taste like sugar—it means it's going to taste like blackberries would taste like, not what sugar would taste like. If we can differentiate between sugar and tastes of fruit, we would all understand wine a little better.

Sweet wine does have the taste of sugar. So when we are tasting a great late harvest wine, and taste the apricot, peaches, and lime, we also get—sugar! Wow! This is what I had in mind. Ah yes, but man does not live by sugar alone. So, expect some of the subtle nuances of fruit—but like real maple syrup, not all tastes are dependent on sugar for flavor—we just got used to it that way.

Next will be earth flavors like minerals and flint and stone. What can we compare these flavors to? Chicken. No. Well, what gives us the familiarity and good feeling of chicken, but taken out of the context of fowl and put into the context of earth, what can we call upon to give us a positive connotation associated with minerals and stone and flint.

Well, lets see. How about mushrooms! They are kind of earthy and minerally and flinty, and for most of us conjure up positive feelings and suggest a flavor concept we can apply to the wine.

See how easy this is? Gives you an appetite and taste for wine, doesn't it. Pinot Noirs are often said to have a "bacony" flavor with overtones of cherries. Sounds delicious doesn't it? Just remember, though, there are hints of bacon—not gobs, and the cherries will not be laden with sugar—the wine will have the taste of cherries, not sugar.

Old Italians (wines that is) will have a taste of hay and manure, and the term we give to this is barnyard. It really does taste this way. Not a particularly appetizing comparison, but when you taste an old Italian with this flavor, you'll swear you're walking through the bull exhibit at the county fair.

Once you become familiar with these flavors, and used to them, you will actually look forward to experiencing them in other red wines. The first time I tasted a great old Cabernet that had a touch of barnyard, I was so excited! "There's that flavor again!" And now we've tasted it in a number of wines, and instead of tasting like unfamiliar shit, it tastes like familiar shit. Ah wine.

As the language of our wine knowledge continues to grow, we will make connections with flavors that we taste in one red wine, to flavors we taste in others. These familiar flavors, combined with new flavors continue to increase our wine vocabulary and knowledge. A wine is like a symphony—so many beautiful sounds—some we can distinguish, others we try to understand, but it is not until some one else makes a connection for us that we fully understand.

Ironstone Vineyards in Murphys, California has a distinctive leather and tobacco flavor to their wines. These flavors are cherished among old Bordeaux, but in a California wine that is a fraction of the price of Bordeaux, they are a real find. But, you have to tell people that they will taste in these wines leather and tobacco. If not, and they are unfamiliar with these tastes, they might make a negative connection.

So many California cabs have the happy berry flavors that the brooding darker flavors may come as a surprise. But these types of flavors are what makes drama and great plays so profound. They have depth and dimension. And they are difficult to understand, and, like God, they are not wholly and all at once perceived and understood. You do have to work at them. That's what makes wine so interesting.

Wine also has a texture or a "feel." Remember a few years back they were talking about substituting all the meat in hot dogs with a meat-like substance, but it had to have good "mouthfeel"? The way we perceive something is not only a direct result of the taste, but of a textural quality as well. How it touches us is important.

So it is with wine. When we first put it into our mouths, do we sense a thin, harsh and austere sensation, or is the wine soft and inviting, full and round and voluptuous. These textural sensations provide a lot of wine's pleasures. If they are absent, or present a negative quality, we enjoy the wine less.

What makes wine thin, compared to full and round? How concentrated the juice is, is one aspect of body. If, for example, the yield from a vineyard is very high because the winemaker is going for quantity and not quality, he may harvest 5 or 6 tons per acre. The juice would be less concentrated and therefore not have as much body. Old vines, and vineyards pruned to give 2 or 3 tons per acre would usually have a fuller body, depending, of course, upon the growing conditions that season.

If it rained right before harvest, the grapes would suck up all the moisture and dilute the juice. This would give the wine a thinner and more austere taste. If the growing season was hot and dry with sun and little rain right up until harvest, then the juice would be more concentrated, and have fuller body.

Also, grapes planted where they are stressed gives a much fuller-bodied wine. So there are a number of reasons why wine may feel differently.

Some wines are not filtered or fined. This will also add to the amount of sediment in the wine. You may feel some slightly sandy particles on your teeth and tongue. These usually dissolve rapidly, and you hardly notice that they are there after a while.

Filtering and fining strips wines of all its flavor. The wines appear to be very clean and bright and sparkling, but they are totally eviscerated at this point, and absent of all the stuff that gives wine its character. Learn to drink wine that is not filtered; you'll get used to it after a while. It will be like getting used to not having your mouth coated with sugar. It will be like tasting fruit—not syrupy imitation flavors.

Educate your palate to appreciate products that must be consumed with a minium of manipulation or adulteration. We have just been so used to refined, manufactured products that whole foods seem unfamiliar to us.

The whole food industry, however, is going back to basics. Interestingly, at the same time when wine has been discovered, like whole foods, to be vastly superior in health benefits and taste. So reeducating ourselves to taste things as they are naturally is worth the time and effort.

Need some help with this? Plant a garden. You will be amazed at how rich and delicious fresh corn is—or fresh asparagus—both eaten raw. Fresh tomatoes picked at the peak of ripeness and new potatoes—that wonderful earthy flavor. Big blackberries bursting with juice. Strawberries that fill your mouth with one bite. Fresh snap peas.

All these flavors are there out in the earth. Like God's grace, we have to want to appreciate and to have them. It is for our benefit and edification that we understand nature and what she provides for us everyday. Learning how to find these treasures and how to enjoy the fruits of the earth, like wine, are one of the true joys of life.

Tasting wine, then, is somewhat of a spiritual experience. We physically ingest the wine, but its texture and flavor and soul are what moves us to feel like we have undergone a religious experience. It moves and breathes and evolves. It lives within us, and brings us its gifts of pleasure and health.

Terms most commonly associated with wine

Balance. When no aspect of wine—either the amount of alcohol, fruit, acid, or oak is so overpowering that it is apparent above all other components.

Harmony. When texture, amount of oak, tannin, acid, fruit, alcohol, body, etc., compliment each other to the point of presenting the wine in a fashion that one feels as if he is listening to a 150 piece orchestra when he sips the wine.

Body. Viscosity of the wine itself. If it is heavy-bodied, the wine feels more dense in your mouth. Lighter bodied wines feel thin and more austere.

Forward. A wine is said to be forward when it shows a lot of the pleasing components early on. A very tannicy wine usually binds a lot of these flavor components so that the wine will need to be aged before it can show well.

Backward. A wine is said to be backward when it is too young, or still needs to be aged so that the tannin will release more of the flavors on your palate. Tight is a similar term.

Fat or Flabby. Wines with little acid have no snap or crispness to them. They just kind of lay in your mouth. These wines are said to be fat or flabby.

Tart, crisp, snappy, lively. All refer to a wine with good acid content.

Aftertaste. The taste that lingers after the wine is swallowed. Wines that leave the essence of what they were behind, or that even taste better after they are swallowed have a good aftertaste. This is usually the mark of a good wine, unless the aftertaste is funky or tastes like an old sock.

Oaky. The sometimes not so subtle flavor of the oak barrel aging that winemakers use to round off the corners of the wine. Oak makes wine more harmonious and soft, and adds a richness to the wine. Sometimes it is overdone and you can taste nothing but oak.

Corked. The unmistakable taste of a damp, wet, musty, basement that occurs when wine has a bad cork.

Complex. When a wine has a lot to offer, and the flavor of the wine changes for the better at each sip, revealing subtle nuances and layers of fruit that increase in richness as the wine is being consumed.

Simple. When a wine tastes the same at each sip, and shows no real layering and dimension. Simple wines are usually inexpensive quaffers that you don't need to think about.

Hardy. Full-bodied and packed with flavor.

Varietal. A wine of at least 75% of the grape variety that is stated on the label.

Light. Little tannin, if any, and simple fruit. Does not refer to alcohol content.

Earthy. When a wine tastes more like tobacco, coffee, chocolate and leather than it does like fruit.

Fruity. When a wine tastes more like fruit that it does like earth.

Tannicy. When a wine has a lot of tannins and you can feel them on your teeth and tongue.

Finish. The sensation or feeling you have about the wine after it is swallowed. If, after you swallow the wine, it's as if you had nothing in your mouth, the wine has a short finish. If, after you swallow, you taste this huge expanse of flavor that coats your mouth and continues to increase each second, the wine has a long finish. If, after you swallow the wine, your mouth tastes very dry and bitter, the wine has a dry finish.

Up Front Flavors. Wines that have a lot of up front flavors usually taste good as soon as you put the wine in your mouth. You will get this big flush of fruit, or earth, and then the wine will dissipate rather quickly.

Structure. Wines with good structure have enough alcohol, acid, and tannin to both hold the wine together for aging, and act as a vehicle to preserve, enhance, and present the flavors harmoniously when consumed.

What Wine Should Not Taste Like

Wine should not taste like old tents, wet basements, vinegar, or medicine. Although it will take some time getting used to, you will know the extent of what a wine should taste like by drinking different wines, especially of different ages, since old wines definitely taste different as they evolve.

What You Should Look For

When swirling an older wine, you will probably notice that the edges may be a bit lighter, or that they may be orange in color. To see this better, tip the glass so that the wine comes about three quarters of the way up the glass, and hold the glass against a white background. You will be able to see the edges pretty plainly. If the edges are a bold plum or deep ruby, the wine is pretty young, or still has some time left to age. If the wine looks watery or bright orange, it is probably getting a little tired. Italian wines however, have an orange or brick color to them when they are quite young, especially wines made from the grape variety Sangiovese.

REVIEW AND REITERATION
INTRODUCTION

■ A connoisseur is simply a person who likes wine, and has an opinion.

■ Tasting wine requires becoming familiar with the tastes you experience. If you drink wine everyday, you will quickly gain knowledge about wine.

■ Try to educate yourself before really getting into tasting, so that you won't be turned off by something totally unexpected.

■ Although wine will taste like fruit, in a lot of cases it will be the taste of fruit, without the sugar.

■ Educate your palate to accept natural products and tastes like those found in wine and whole foods. If you're used to putting sugar on everything and love white bread, and think that ketchup is a vegetable, you might need to do some work on your palate before enjoying whole and natural products like wine.

■ Wine is not only tasted in our mouth, but in our head. As wine vaporizes and the ethers waft up the back of our throats into our sinuses, our olfactory sense goes to work analyzing the wine and feeding the information, along with our taste buds, into the brain.

■ The concept of flavor is what is important. Try to compare what you are tasting to something that is known, or in your experience.

■ The range of what good wine tastes like is astronomical, and it will take some time for you to understand and realize all the flavors and nuances possible in a glass of wine.

■ Wine also has a texture. The "feel" of a wine is determined by its body or viscosity, the amount of tannin, and the conditions of the growing season that year. It also depends on the variety of grape being used, and if the wine is fined or filtered.

■ Planting a garden and getting used to fresh flavors is a good way to enjoy wholesome natural products. It will help you understand the range of flavors in a glass of wine.

■ Tasting wine is a spiritual as well as mental and physical experience.

■ Wine should not taste like old tents, wet basements, or vinegar.

■ Look at the edges of a glass of wine to determine the amount of aging it can undergo. The deeper and darker, the more you can allow the other bottles of the same year of that brand to age in your cellar. If you notice very light or watery edges, or an orange color, and its not a Chianti or Brunello, you better drink the rest of these in your cellar.

PART ONE

The Basics: Procedures, Terms & Definitions of Winemaking

PRONUNCIATION GUIDE
PART ONE

Muscat (mus-cot)
A grape variety used in making sweet wines such as Asti Spumante.

Brix level (briks)
A degree of sugar in grapes.

Riesling (ree´- sling)
Grape variety used in making excellent sweet and dry wines. Germany's #1 grape variety.

Chenin Blanc (shenin-blahnc)
Grape variety that makes very pleasant lightly sweet wines.

Chaptilization (chap ta la zay´ shun)
process of adding sugar to wine.

Chardonnay (shar doe nay´)
Great white grape variety of California, Burgundy, and Champagne.

PART ONE

The Basics: Procedures, Terms & Definitions of Winemaking

. . . .

The main ingredient in grape wine is, of course, grapes. The grape vine is a veritable storehouse of energy. One vine, if allowed to grow wild, would eventually cover an acre of land! Providing nutrients for this plant is an extensive root system.

When grape vines are planted on slopes, and on poorer soils, the vines are stressed and the root system scavenges for food. In this hunt, roots may reach down over 100 feet, and literally pick up nutrients from layers of earth that are tens of thousands of years old. Grapes produced on these stressed vines are of greater character than grapes grown on wet or fertile soil, because there is less water in them, and therefore the juice is more concentrated.

The deep root system also supplies the grape with a plethora of minerals, elements, compounds and substances that the earth has been digesting for eons. These compounds end up in the inside of the grape skin called the tannin, and during fermentation when the cap (collection of crushed skins) is continually punched down into the juice, this tannin intermingles with the pulp and liquid from the grape.

Tannin is usually a bit puckery and causes a kind of "tannic grip" that you can feel on your teeth and tongue. Tannin causes red wine to be red, and gives red wine its ability to age. In fact, the more tannin, the more potential a wine has of extended aging.

Over a period of years, the tannin begins to break down, and slowly adds its compounds to the wine. As the tannin dissolves, the wine becomes softer, more easily drunk, and develops a myriad of flavors. Red wines consumed too quickly after bottling and not allowed to age can be a bit tannicy or "grippy." Red wine is usually much better when aged.

If grape vines are planted on soils that receive a lot of rain, or, are very wet, the grapes usually end up gorged with water. This dilutes the juice, and causes a stunted root system that does not go in search of nutrients. The result is a rather watery wine with no real flavor and complexity.

In general, the closer to harvest that it rains, the more diluted the juice. Most of the best soils for grape vines then, are stony and rocky slopes that receive most of their water at bud (Spring).

This area should also have a sunny growing period with warm days and cool nights, and a growing season long enough for good "hang time" (a period of time long enough for the grapes to develop fully and ripen before harvest). Harvest should be warm and dry, so that the grapes do not develop rots and funguses.

Areas throughout the United States with such climates include California and Washington, and some of the areas in Oregon. Other states might have similar conditions—like some of the states in the east—but the harsh winters and low temperatures either kill the vines that make the best wine, or, at least kill the buds.

Areas outside the United States producing great wine are: France, Italy, Australia, Chili, Spain, Portugal, Germany, and to a lesser extent, but definitely improving, New Zealand, South Africa, and Argentina.

How wine is made

Wine is simply fermented fruit juice. Every year in the fall, grapes are harvested when the sun has ripened them to the desired degree of sweetness and ripeness. The degree of sweetness in a grape is called its Brix level. Wine grapes are picked at 21 to 23 degrees brix. In contrast, grapes bought for munching and snacking are usually about 15 to 17 degree brix, so wine grapes are much sweeter than table grapes. After harvest, grapes are quickly brought to the winery and put into de-stemmers and crushers, where the stems are removed and the grapes are crushed to release their juice.

In red wine, the color is obtained by leaving the skins of the red grape in contact with the juice—for whatever amount of time the winemaker desires—this is called contact time. This creates the color and adds flavor—the longer the contact time, and the hotter the fermentation up to a point (after about 89 or 90 degrees the yeast will die and fermentation will stop) the more intense the wine will be; extraction is very complete at this point, and the wines will have all the tannin of the grape. To make white wine, all the skins and the stems are removed, and the juice is pumped from one tank to another—this is called racking.

At this point, yeast is added, and fermentation begins. During fermentation, red wine must be continually stirred to make sure the cap is in contact with the juice. The cap, the collection of crushed skins, is pushed down into the wine, over and over again. Fermentation takes place over the next few weeks in stainless steel tanks.

The winemaker constantly tests for sugar, alcohol, acid, and color—he can stop the process at any time—when all the sugar is turned into alcohol we say that the wine is bone dry—most reds are bone dry. Or, the winemaker may leave anywhere from just a speck of residual sugar—like some Chardonnays are made to cover up a slight tendency to finish bitter—to quite a bit of residual sugar for Rieslings, Muscats, and dessert wines. Residual sugar is sugar not turned into alcohol, and left in the wine.

Sometimes wine is put through a secondary fermentation process called malo-lactic fermentation. In this process, bacteria turns malic acid—the tart acid of apples—into lactic acid— the creamy and smooth acid of butter. White wines become mellow and very rich and expansive. Red wines become less astringent. Sometimes the wine is filtered.

> **CONSUMER TIP**
>
> Wine tastes are fun and entertaining ways to learn about the attributes of different wines. Either get on a mailing list of your local store, or start a tasting group of your own. Have a theme for the night— either red or white or dry or sweet— anything you like—and have each person attending bring a bottle that fits the theme.
>
> Taste the wines in flights of two or three, so that you can compare all the wines and decide what you like and why. Go around the table and ask each person to give a few comments on the wine, and why he/she likes it or doesn't like it.
>
> People will learn from each other. Invite somebody knowledgeable and have the group listen to her comments. The only items you will need are three glasses per person—so you can taste three wines at a time—a "dump" bucket to pour out unwanted portions of wine, and a water pitcher to rinse the glasses for the next flight. Ask you local merchant for suggestions and ideas, or just invite him over.
>
> Try to make some wine yourself! There are various kits which will allow you to make about 5 gallons of wine right in your own home. All the equipment is supplied, and its much less work than you'd think. It's just as much fun, and less work, than a garden.You'll learn a lot.

This process, however, is falling out of practice since it strips the wine of most of its unique and subtle flavors. After fermentation, the wine is now ready for aging. Most aging is done in oak barrels. Oak aging does for wine what cooking over a wood fire does for food—it enhances its flavors and allows the components to develop into a harmonious whole. Aging can take anywhere from eight months for whites, to 36 months for some reds like the Italian Barolos and Amarones. After this, the wine is bottled and brought to the store.

Sweetness and dryness

A lot of people who don't drink wine when asked why will say that it tastes sour or bitter. These people have only sampled some of the dry reds and whites on the market, and obviously haven't been exposed to the plethora of soft and semi-sweet wines available from the local stores. It is up to the retailer to discern the tastes of the customer, and selling them a bottle of wine before ascertaining this information has turned many would be wine enthusiasts away from the wine store and away from wine.

Muscats, Rieslings, Chenin Blancs, and all German wines are delicately to very sweet, and very easy to drink. But what do you look for, and how can these wines be found? In the supermarket, you have to know your wines, but a good wine shop with a tasting bar is the place you will find a good wine. When you walk into the wine shop, don't be intimidated. I don't care if you are a doctor, a lawyer, or a banker with an I.Q. of over 200, you are probably not going to be as knowledgeable about a wine as someone who has spent great deals of time around salespeople, tasting rooms, thousands of samples, and frequent trips to the wine growing areas themselves; it's impossible to keep up unless you are around it continually.

Would the retailer know your profession? Would you let him fill your tooth, operate on your heart, or know the intricacies of banking, the stock market, politics, etc., etc., etc.? Of course not. Let him, or her, help you make a selection. Let them know you are interested, and they know they will have a good friend and a good customer.

If you like sweet whites, don't be afraid to ask for them. Sweet wines are the first step to serious wine drinking. If the retailer has a tasting area, she will be able to discover where your tastes lie, and which degree of sweetness is comfortable for you. And, after a few questions about a price range that is comfortable, you should be on your way with a bottle of wine that you'll enjoy.

"Bone Dry" simply means that all the sugar has been turned into alcohol. If a wine is said to be "dry," and not "bone-dry," then all the sugar has not been turned into alcohol. This residual sugar, in small quantities will not make the wine sweet, only less tart. If a wine is semi-sweet or semi-dry, more sugar is left in the wine. The winemaker must have a certain level of alcohol in the wine— remember, that wine is simply fruit, and if there is not enough sugar, acid and alcohol (these are natural preservatives), the fruit will eventually decompose, and the wine will fall apart.

So if the alcohol level can not be reached with the degree of sugar that the winemaker must have to achieve the desired taste, he must wait until later in the year to pick the grapes; these "late harvest" grapes contain more sugar. The winemaker also may simply add more sugar to the grape juice prior to fermentation; this is called chaptilization. Very sweet wines like Ports and Sherries are fortified with high alcohol brandy. Port and Sherry will warm you up rather quickly.

Red wines are usually fermented bone dry—all the sugar has been turned into alcohol. Add to this fact that most red wines contain quite a bit of tannin, and you can see why it is more difficult to enjoy red wines at first than it is some of the other softer, less tannicy, sweet white wines. Chardonnays are also fermented bone dry. It is rather common place now, however, to leave just a bit of residual sugar in Chardonnays. This small amount causes the wine to finish smoother.

Chardonnays have a slight tendency to have a bitter finish at times. Oak aging also rounds out the flavors of bone dry wines. The rich and mellow flavors of oak really enhance a wine—as long as the winemaker doesn't overdo it so that all that you're tasting is oak—and no fruit. Some wineries have discovered a technique that gives their wine oak flavor without paying the enormous price of oak barrels, which significantly increases the price. They are adding shredded oak chips. These cuttings are simply allowed to soak in the wine for a period of time, and then they are removed. The result is a wine that has oak flavor without the cost of actually spending the time and money for true oak aging.

Is it as good as aging wine for months in expensive barrels as the wine evolves and matures? I don't think I need to answer that question. If, because of the greater health benefits of red wine, you prefer to drink it, even if it is unpleasant for you, rather than the softer and sweeter Rieslings, Muscats, and Chenin Blancs, there is something that you can do to modify the dry taste of reds, and that is to mix something with them.

A lot of people add a little bit of Port or Sherry to their red wine. This will sweeten it a little, and make it more palatable. Add as much or as little as you like. Some add Muscat to their red wines—in fact, because most Muscats are lower in alcohol—some actually as low as 4%, you may substantially lower the alcohol content. Both my great-grandmother and my grandmother added "7-Up" to their red wine, because the red wines that came out of our family's old whiskey barrels were a bit strong for them. They may have invented the first wine cooler! I know this last bit of information has made some wine aficionados cringe, but a first step is a first step.

REVIEW AND REITERATION
PART ONE

- Character is a term applied to grapes grown from stressed vines. These vines, planted on sloped and stoney or rocky soils, must work hard to search for nutrients and water. The resultant grapes have less liquid content, and more concentrated pulp. The amount of grapes is also less per vine. Further concentrating the nutrients and compounds in a smaller number of grapes. The wine made from these grapes is richer, tastier, and of better quality.

- Tannin is a substance that forms on the inside of the grape skin, and is also part of the skin make-up. Compounds furnished by the roots are stored in the tannin. To make red wine, grapes are destemmed and crushed, and soaked with the tannin, allowing it to dissolve and work into the juice during fermentation. A lot of the health benefits of red wine come from these compounds. Tannins also allow red wine to age, slowly releasing compounds as the wine continues to evolve and mature. Tannins are also responsible for the grippy feeling on your teeth and tongue, but in older wines, the tannins are much softer allowing the wines to be mellow and rich; young red wines tend to be more tannic.

- "Cap" is the accumulated skins that float to the top of the tank during fermentation. The cap must be either mechanically pushed down into the juice over and over, or, the juice itself must be continually pulled from the bottom of the tank via hose or the like, and deposited on the cap, causing the tannins to be mixed with the juice. The cap is removed after fermentation.

■ Fermentation is the process of allowing the yeast present in the wine naturally, or the added cultured yeast, to turn the sugar in the juice into alcohol. Also in this process, other activity is taking place that is breaking down the compounds in the grape skins and imparting these to the juice. Fermentation is constantly being checked by the winemaker. If he wants a bone dry wine— such as most reds are, he will allow all the sugar to be turned into alcohol, and no residual sugar will be left. If the winemaker wants his wines to be just dry, he will stop fermentation with a bit of residual sugar, or, before all of the sugar is turned into alcohol. The sweeter the wine, the more residual sugar will be left in the wine.

Note: If the winemaker wants very sweet wine, and there is not enough sugar to have the proper amount of alcohol, which forms the basic structure of the wine and allows it to age properly, he must either add sugar (chaptilization) or pick grapes with a very high sugar content. Such grapes are picked late in the year—they are called late harvest, and the sugar content is as high as any dried fruit.

■ Brix level. The degree of sweetness in a grape. Most wines need grapes to be about 21 to 23 degrees brix to make a good wine with adequate alcohol. Alcohol preserves the fruit.

■ Bone dry is a term applied to wine in which all the sugar is turned into alcohol.

■ Dry is a term applied to wine in which a small amount of residual sugar is left in the wine.

■ Semi-dry (or semi-sweet) and sweet, are terms applied to wine in which progressively more residual sugar is left in the wine, and not turned into alcohol.

■ Malo-lactic fermentation is not really a fermentation at all, but simply an addition of certain strain of bacteria which turns the malic acid (the acid of apples) into lactic acid (the acid of butter). In this process, some of the flavor of the fruit is lost, and a buttery flavor becomes more predominant. A winemaker, not to lose all the fruit in exchange for butter, will therefore blend wine which has gone under malo-lactic fermentation with wine that has not, to get the proper balance of fruit and butter. You might see, therefore, 50% malolactic fermentation, or 70% malolactic fermentation etc., on the label, referring to the final blend. Wines which do not undergo this malolactic fermentation are very snappy, crisp, lively, spritey, tart, and have a lot of fresh fruit flavors.

REVIEW AND REITERATION
PART ONE

- Fining is the process of adding egg whites to the wine, and the bigger particles are attracted to them, and then the egg whites are removed with the attached particles. This is the most unobtrusive way to cleanse the wine, while leaving a lot of the substance in the wine to give it flavor and character. Sediment will form in the bottles of wine that is only fined. This is the mark of a well-made wine, and not "junk" left in a dirty bottle.

- Filtering is an intrusive way of removing particles from the wine. It, in effect, strips the wine of the substances that give it all its flavor. The wine is very clear, and almost sparkles. But, the taste is denuded and the wine is basically eviscerated and devoid of all the compounds that made it what it is. It's like making stew, and then straining out all the meat and vegetables. This practice is falling out with most winemakers who make serious wine. Consumers, however, must be educated that a clear wine, doesn't denote a better wine, just a filtered one.

- Aging is a process in which the wine is allowed to develop over a period of time. Most wines age at least one year before being bottled—the consumer can age his wine once home in his cellar until the desired maturity.

- Oak aging is the process of aging the wine in expensive oak casks prior to bottling. American white oak and French oak are two popular oaks used for aging. Oak adds a softness to a wine. If the wine does not have a lot of character or flavor, too much oak aging will overpower the wine, and the wine will be said to be out of balance, or, over oaked. Generally speaking, red wines are oaked more than white wines because red wines can absorb more oak without getting out of balance. Some white wines have so much oak you could build a house with them.

- Chaptilization is the process of adding sugar to the grape juice prior to fermentation. This is done either because the grapes do not have enough sugar at harvest to produce the required amount of alcohol, or, because the winemaker needs a certain amount of residual sugar to remain after the desired alcohol level is reached, and the brix level at harvest is too low to supply the sugar needed.

PART TWO

How to Pair Wine & Food

PRONUNCIATION GUIDE
PART TWO

Bordeaux (bor doe´)
Great winemaking region in France.

Cabernet Sauvignon
(cab er nay´ saw vin yawn´)
Great red grape variety of California and
Bordeaux, France.

PART TWO

How to Pair Wine and Food

It is almost impossible to talk about wine out of the context of food. Wine enhances the taste of food, and food enhances the taste of wine. There is definitely a synergistic effect between the two. Why?

There are certain elements, compounds, flavors, textures, etc. in food that have a definite impact on your taste buds and in your mouth. For example, a rich and buttery cream sauce has a tendency to coat your palate, and, after a while you need to have something clean your mouth. That dry white wine that was too astringent by itself now has a real duty: it cuts through the heavy coatings in your mouth and refreshes with its crisp, snappy and clean-tasting flavors—and the rich creamy butter neutralizes the acid in the wine, greatly modifying its taste and allowing it to be more mellow and soft. These two entities have greatly enhanced the taste and effect of each other. Together, being better than each would have been separately.

In addition, there are certain compounds in food that unlock flavors in wine, and, there are certain elements in wine that unlock the flavors in food. So there is not only a textural improvement, but a chemical synergy as well. Red Bordeaux and Cabernet Sauvignons go extremely well with rich meats and hearty stews. These tannins, which can be overpowering without food, now unlock the flavor of the meat that would have been swallowed without ever being noticed—now there is an explosion of flavors as not only the tannins are modified by enzymes in the meat, but as the compounds in the meat allow all the flavors of the wine to be tasted. You really have to experience this unique chemical and textural activity for yourself. Once you experience it, mealtime will take on a whole new meaning.

As far as white wines are concerned, a rich and buttery Chardonnay goes well with the great rich flavors of salmon. Light and crisp wines like Chenin Blanc and Rieslings go well with chicken, vegetables and white meats. If you want a rule, red wines with red meats and hearty stews, and white wines with white meats, vegetables and lighter fare. Most acceptable, however, is to drink what you want with your dinner-as long as you enjoy it. To talk about wine, then, in the absence of food, is difficult at best. It is difficult to go into a store and taste wines and imagine how they will taste with food, but after some practice, you will become very confident about your selections—as long as you remember that you are going to be drinking these wines with food and not by themselves. Now, you don't have to sit down to a full meal to enjoy your wine.

Some bread and cheese with that Chardonnay will be excellent before dinner. And, some pasta and beans, or, pasta and vegetables with a glass of Riesling will do more for you than you can imagine. Going to use the grill for a quick snack of fish or grilled vegetables, or whatever? Then there's a wine for that also. Wine is good for you; it is good food.

Don't feel guilty about drinking wine—just treat it like everything else in a well thought-out lifestyle, and that is to eat and drink heartily, but in moderation, always aware that excess in even the healthiest of substances is never smart. Another aspect of wine and food combination that is sometimes overlooked—probably more so in the United States than abroad—is our state of mind during meals. So many times the activities of the day become the focus, that relaxing during mealtime is almost impossible.

We eat standing over the sink, or try to close a business deal rather than enjoy the food and the company. We eat on the run because there isn't enough time in the day, and fast food restaurants become very convenient to help speed us on our way to the grave. The opportunity to sit down and drink wine with dinner at home is becoming a precious memory. Dinners planned around everyone being home and eating together have become the exception rather than the rule.

One of the best stress busters around is to sit down to a good meal with family and friends, great food, and wine. Indeed, it has been documented that our immune system's response to invading germs is highly activated when one partakes of a tasty well prepared meal, in which the wine plays a part in the gastronomic pleasure of the entire eating experience.

Simply put, you are much less likely to get sick if you relax with good food and wine and totally enjoy the experience. The reason? First of all, stress is reduced, and when stress is reduced, your body functions more efficiently. Secondly, the sensory pleasure of a tasty, well-prepared hot meal steps up the immune response; this has been documented.

And, third, components in the wine known to have beneficial effects not only by themselves, but in concert with nutrients from food, give both the body and mind strength and dynamism to tackle everyday stresses and chores. Taking time to eat and enjoy food has become a lost art; it has slipped by the wayside and is blasted from our daily agenda because it is looked at as wasteful and not important enough.

Also seen as unimportant is the family sitting down together, parents discussing the days activities with the children, and the children learning to share their experiences, hopes, fears, and joys with the people most important to them. The children also learn to put things in perspective. That there is a time for work, and a time for play. A time to work as hard as your can, and a time to back away and smell the roses.

It is much easier dealing with problems when there is a good support system at home, but this does not just happen. It takes a great amount of thought and discipline to compartmentalize

CONSUMER TIP

Wine is the healthiest mealtime beverage you can consume. It not only is good for you, but actually makes what you are eating taste better. Instead of taking meals on the run, maybe try eating later, when the whole family is out of all the activities of the day. Just having dinner at 6:30 or 7:00 p.m. instead of 5:00 p.m., will probably allow the whole family to be together to talk, discuss the problems and share the delights of the day with each other. At this time of night, it is also very conducive for wine to be consumed.

Try enjoying wine with your family by adding a little water or 7-Up to the younger children's wine, and they can enjoy their wine, while you are enjoying yours. This not only teaches children that wine is a healthy food, but gets them used to drinking wine in the home.

When wine is treated like a drug, it is consumed in mass quantities outside the home, usually in groups of teens who binge for the effect and end up not knowing when to stop. You wouldn't let your kid drive the car without proper knowledge, teach him the proper way to enjoy and consume wine—it will enhance the quality and quantity of the lives of all the family.

Thoughtful consideration, trust and love, and sharing God's gifts to us is what family life is all about. Take advantage of the good things he has provided for us.

activities so that some do not overrun and spoil all the others. Worry is easy. It is the result of lack of faith in yourself, in God, in your lifestyle. It is the inability to put to rest things that should be put to rest.

So we have lost more than the enjoyment of life and good wine and good food; we have lost the way. The incidence of heart disease, cancer, and a host of other maladies begins to overtake us. We feel unequal to the task, and tired heart muscles give way, or the mind begins to turn the body off. We have feelings that our growth and fulfillment are stunted—so growth takes place in other physical and unnatural ways, and cancer begins to invade our body.

You eat to get filled up, you sleep because its time; the alarm rings and it starts all over. What we have lost has been tremendous. The alcohol in wine is there for a reason. It makes you stop and relax. There are some people who don't drink wine because they say it makes them sleepy—well, that's the idea. Where the idea came that your life must be filled from dusk to dawn with work and that this Spartan ideal is the proper way to live is beyond me.

It is a sick existence. If one really gets into the wine-food-life-experience, he or she will find that the fullness and richness of a lifestyle well ordered and thought out is not only much more compassionate, but life as it was intended to be. The simple pleasures and love and joy of family, of friends, of God, and of life, is life. And to fill it with endless activities and think that your getting somewhere is a foolish existence. Ernest Hemingway said it best "Never confuse movement with action."

Wine relaxes, nourishes you with its fruit, caresses you with its flavors and aroma. It is from the earth, and will, with the food become a part of you. Wine, Benjamin Franklin said, "is proof positive that God loves us and wants to keep us happy." Amen.

REVIEW AND REITERATION
PART TWO

- The effects of food & wine consumed together are synergistic; one enhances and compliments the taste of the other, making each taste better together than they would separately.

- A crisp, snappy, and dry white wine will compliment a rich buttery and creamy sauce by cutting through the rich layers of fats and oils to cleanse the palate, and the creams and fats in the sauce will mute and lessen the effects of the acids in a snappy and crisp dry white, making it softer, rounder, and mellower.

- Dry red wine enhances the flavors of red meat and hearty stews. The tannins in the wine are softened by components in the meat, and the acids and tannins in the wine will make meat taste more flavorful.

- White wines usually go well with white meats, chicken vegetables, and fish. Red wines go well with red meats and hearty stews and sauces. Or, just drink your favorite wine with your favorite food.

- Sweet dessert wines go well with fresh fruit, mousse, chocolate, and a variety of desserts; experiment!

- Drinking wine with meals reduces stress and allows one the time and atmosphere to eat slowly and enjoy the flavors of the food.

- Eating flavorful food enhanced by wine strengthens the immune system; this is a documented fact.

- There are components in wine that act individually and in concert with components in food to protect your body from cholesterol, high blood pressure, and free radicals which cause disease.

- The alcohol in wine relaxes you, and lessens inhibitions.

- Wine is the traditional mealtime beverage; it has been consumed with food down through the ages, and enjoyed and appreciated properly, will add immeasurably to the quality and quantity of your life.

PART THREE

The Great Winemaking Grapes

PRONUNCIATION GUIDE
PART THREE

Merlot (mer low´)
Big, fat, soft, fleshy grape used to make soft and gracious red wines.

Pinot Noir (pee´ no N'War´)
Outstanding grape variety used in Burgundy, Champagne, and California.

Zinfandel (zin fen del´)
Red grape used to make a soft rosé wine that is slightly sweet called White Zinfandel, and, used to make excellent dry red wines—Zinfandel is indigenous to California.

Sangiovese (san gee o vay´ see)
Red grape of Italy used to make Chianti, Brunello di Montalcino, and Vino Nobile di Montepulciano. All of the region called Tuscany.

Nebbiolo (neb ee o´ low)
Red grape variety of the Piedmont region in Italy used in making Italy's most intense and richest red wines. They are: Barolo, Barbaresco, and Gattinara.

Sauvignon Blanc (saw vin yawn blahnc)
White grape variety of Bordeaux, France used both to make dry and sweet wines. Very susceptible to Botrytis Cinerea because of its thin skin. This makes it perfect for dessert wines which need this "noble rot" for outstanding depth of flavor.

Semillon (sem ee own´)
White grape variety that is used with Sauvignon Blanc to make Bordeaux's best dry and sweet wines. Very suseptible to Botrytis Cinerea because of its thin skin.

Syrah (seer ah)
Red grape variety that makes some of Australia's greatest wines.

PART THREE

The Great Winemaking Grapes

We are going to limit our discussion to the most important grapes used in winemaking. There are many other grapes that we could mention that are used in small amounts in blending, but at this point they will confuse rather than educate. The major discussion, then, will be on the grapes that make the best, and the most wine. For red wine, these are Cabernet Sauvignon, Merlot, Pinot Noir, Zinfandel, Sangiovese, and Nebbiolo. For white wine, these grapes are Chardonnay, Riesling, Sauvignon Blanc and Semillon.

The red grapes

Cabernet Sauvignon is a dark, small, thick-skinned grape capable of making the world's greatest wines. It is the main red grape of California, and it is the predominant red grape in the Bordeaux region in France. Its thick skin allows tannin content to be rather high, and this gives a wine great ageability. The flavor of Cabernet is reminiscent of blackberries, with hints of leather, tobacco, and chocolate. These earth flavors give complexity to the fruit and make the wines from it quite profound.

Merlot is a big, fat, soft, fleshy grape capable of making very soft and graceful wines—although, because of the thinner skin and consequent limited tannins, not as ageworthy as Cabernet. It is one of the most important grapes of California, and the second most important grape variety—next to Cabernet Sauvignon—in Bordeaux, France. Merlot is often blended with Cabernet to make it softer and moderate its tannins. Merlot is quite productive, ripens early, and has lately been bottled by itself to provide exceptionally soft red wines.

Pinot Noir is probably the most distinguished of the red grape varieties because it makes wines with outstanding flavor and great finesse. It is the red grape of Burgundy, France, and in California, once the idiosyncrasies of the grape were figured out, has started to make some exceptionally fine red wine. A great Pinot Noir or Red Burgundy will have flavors of bacon cooking, with overtones of cherries. Pinot Noir is also responsible for about 50% of all the Champagne from the Champagne region of France;

together with Chardonnay, all Champagnes, must, by law, be made with these two grapes.

Zinfandel is indigenous to California, and grows nowhere else in the world. The Primo-Tivo grape of Italy is thought to be an ancestor, however. This grape was making very nice red table wines until about the mid seventies when it was discovered that it made a quite tasty, soft and delicious Rosé called White Zinfandel. By lessening the contact time with the skin, a light pink color was obtained instead of the normal dark red. This also eliminated most of the bitter tannins. Also, residual sugar was allowed, and the resultant wine revolutionized the wine market in California. Red Zinfandel is peppery and tastes of dewberries. It also is usually higher in alcohol content. White Zinfandel is delicately sweet, pink in color, and tastes of strawberries and melons.

Sangiovese. Great red grape of Italy, used in making Chianti, Brunello di Montalcino, and Vino Nobile di Montepulciano. It has a crisp, tart, cherry flavor, and is light to medium-bodied.

Nebbiolo. The other great red grape of Italy. Nebbiolo makes some of the most intense red wines in the world. They are extremely long lived. They are Barolo, Barbaresco, and Gattinara.

Syrah makes a fragrant and flavorful wine in America, Australia, and France. Sometimes it is called Shiraz. Not to be confused however with Petite Sirah which is another variety altogether.

White wine grapes

Chardonnay. Chardonnay is the aristocrat of white wine grapes. In France it produces all the great White Burgundies, including Chablis, Montrachet, Pouilly-Fuisse, and along with Pinot Noir, are the main grapes of Champagne. It yields small amounts per acre, but is planted extensively in California where it is the number-one selling white wine. Chardonnay has very good acid content, and very good sugar content—these two compounds are essential in making world class wines. Acid holds wine together giving a framework on which the fruit must build. Sugar is turned into alcohol, and alcohol is the other component on which a serious wine is built. Also, because of low yields per acre, Chardonnay has excellent concentration and richness.

Riesling. One of the very best white wine grapes ever grown. It is extensively planted in Germany and makes their very best white wines. In

California, it also yields wine of superior flavor and character. It is best grown in stony soil, and on slopes, like most grapes. Again, this stressing of the vine yields the best wine-making grapes. Riesling is usually fermented a little sweet. That is, not all of the sugar is fermented into alcohol. This sugar that is left over is called residual sugar. In Germany, there are different sweetness levels at which you can buy Riesling, all defined on the label. Kabinett is least sweet, spatlese is a little sweeter, auslese sweeter yet. Beerenauslese and trockenbeerenauslese are extremely sweet.

Sauvignon Blanc. An herbal and grassy tasting white grape, that when given oak aging makes a unique and delicious white wine. Some winemakers have their Sauvignon Blanc resemble Chardonnay. Other winemakers keep the herbal and grassy characteristics very apparent, don't use much oak, and therefore make a wine that is very true to the flavor of the grape. A wine made in this way is said to have a lot of varietal flavor, or, true to the variety of grape. Used in Bordeaux to make white wine, usually in a blend with Semillon.

Semillon. A thin-skinned grape very susceptible to Botrytis Cinerea—a fungus which on this grape and Sauvignon Blanc is called the "Noble Rot." Botrytis gives superb honey-apricot and lime nuances to the great Sauternes. Dessert wines of Bordeaux, are the greatest in the world. Semillon is also used in dessert wines in California. It is also fermented dry and sold by the name, if at least 75%, of simply "Semillon." One of the two grapes used to make White Bordeaux—either the dry, or the ones produced in the region of Bordeaux called Sauternes or Barsac, the other grape is, of course, Sauvignon Blanc.

CONSUMER TIP

When having dinners with family and friends, make it a practice to bring wine to the host, and also make it a habit for the host to open everything that is brought to taste! I have been over other's houses for dinner and had my wine put in the closet for another occasion-at this point I kindly ask to taste what I have brought. This gives everyone the pleasure of tasting the wines that they have purchased, and, it gives everyone a chance to taste some different wines with food.

Make it a habit to buy and taste wine wherever and whenever you can. You will be surprised how quickly you learn and are able to discern the different aspects of wine when you consume it often. It's not a sin you know. Christ drank wine.

REVIEW AND REITERATION
PART THREE

■ The most important red wine grapes are Cabernet Sauvignon, Merlot, Pinot Noir, Zinfandel, Sangiovese, Nebbiolo, and Syrah.

■ The most important white wine grapes are Chardonnay, Riesling, Sauvignon Blanc and Semillon.

■ Cabernet Sauvignon makes an intense rich red; it is one of the most important grapes of California, and the main red grape of Bordeaux, France.

■ Merlot makes a softer red, is very important in California, and the second most important red grape variety of Bordeaux, France.

■ Pinot Noir makes a rich and classy red wine in California. It is the number one red wine-making grape in Burgundy, France.

■ Sangiovese and Nebbiolo are the major red grapes of Italy. Sangiovese makes Chianti, Brunello di Montalcino, and Vino Nobile di Montepulciano. Nebbiolo makes probably the most intense red wines in the world. They are Barolo, Barbaresco, and Gattinara.

■ Zinfandel makes a hearty red wine and is indigenous to California, growing nowhere else in the world. It also makes a pleasant and highly popular rosé called White Zinfandel.

■ Chardonnay is the major white wine grape in California, and the major white wine grape in Burgundy, France.

■ Riesling makes dry, semi-sweet, and sweet wines in California, Ohio, New York, and is the major grape variety of Germany.

■ Sauvignon Blanc and Semillon make both dry and sweet wines in California, and in Barsac and Sauternes, France; they make some of the finest sweet wines in the world.

PART FOUR

How a Bottle of Wine Gets Its Name

Varietal (va ri´ e tel)
A wine containing at least 75% of one grape variety.

Meritage (mer´ i tij)
Wine of California that is fashioned after the Bordeaux style of winemaking and uses the grape varieties of that region in the wine, and nothing else. For red wine, these grapes are Cabernet Sauvignon, Merlot, Cabernet Frac, Petite Verdot, and Malbec. For white wine, these grape varieties are Semillon and Sauvignon Blanc.

Cabernet Franc (cab er nay´ frahnc)
One of the five blending grapes of Bordeaux used in making red wine. It is very fruity— sometimes almost vegetal. Used in small quantities.

Petite Verdot (pa teet´ ver doe´)
One of the five blending grapes used in making red Bordeaux.

Malbec (mal bec´)
One of the five blending grapes used in making red Bordeaux. It has a rasberry flavor.

Champagne (sham payn´)
Major sparkling wine region of France.

Burgundy (bur´ gun dee)
Major wine producing area of France.

Rhone Valley (rone)
Wine producing region in France including Gigondas, Chateneuf Du Pape, Cotie Rotie, Hermitage, Condrieu, Tavel, Lirac, etc.

Loire Valley (loo are´)
Wine producing region of France including Pouilly Fume, Sancerre, Vouvray, Chinon, Quincy, Touraine.

Beaujolais (bow zha lay´)
Area of Burgundy, France that makes very light, agreeable red wines from the Gamay grape. Beaujolais nouveau is consumed two moths after being bottled.

Sauternes (saw turns´)
Area in Bordeaux that makes outstanding sweet wine.

Muscadet (mus ca day´)
White grape variety used in the Loire Valley, France.

Chinon (she non´)
Red grape variety used for making wine in the Loire Valley.

Cinsault (sin zoe´)
Red grape variety used for making wine in the Rhone Valley.

Mouvedre (moo ved´ ree)
Red wine making grape of the Rhone Valley.

Grenache (gra nahsh´)
Red wine making grape of the Rhone Valley.

Marsanne (mar sahn´)
White grape of the Rhone Valley.

Rousanne (roo sahn´)
White grape of the Rhone Valley.

Chianti (kee on´ tee)
Red wine of the Tuscany region of Italy using Sangiovese grapes to make their wine.

Brunello di Montalcino
(broo nell´ owe dee mon tal chee´ no)
Specific region of Tuscany, Italy, using the Sangiovese grape.

Vino Nobile di Montepulciano
(vee´ no no ba lay
dee mon tay pull chee ahn´ owe)
Specific area of Tuscany, Italy, using Sangiovese to make their famous red wine.

Barolo (ba ro´ low)
Intense red wine of Piedmont, Italy. Nebbiolo is used to make the wine.

Barbaresco (bar ba res´ ko)
Intense red wine of Piedmont, Italy. The Nebbiolo grape is used to make it.

Gattinara (gah tah nah´ rah)
Red wine made of Nebbiolo grapes.

Valpolicella (val pol i chell´ a)
Red wine making region in Italy making light red wines of the same name.

Bardolino (bar doe lee´ no)
Red wine making region in Italy, making light red wines of the same name.

Lambrusco (lam broo´ sko)
Red wine of Italy making light, slightly sparkling red wine.

Pinot Grigio (pee´ no gree´ jee owe)
White grape of Italy producing dry white wine.

Trebbiano (treb ee ah´ no)
White grape of Italy producing dry white wine.

Asti Spumante (ah´ stee spoo mahn´ tee)
White, sweet, sparkling wine of Asti, Italy, made from the Muscat grape.

Malvasia (mal vah´ jee ah)
Grape variety of Italy making good sweet or dry wine.

Piesporter (peez´ por ter)
Town of Piesport in Germany. -er is German suffix.

Goldtropfchen (gold trop shen)
Famous wine producing vineyard in Germany.

Riesling (ree´ sling)
Great German grape variety.

Spatlese (spot lay´ say)
Level of sweetness in a German grape, one up from the least sweet. This is the level of sweetness in which the grapes were picked—and not the final sweetness level of the wine.

Wehlener (way´ lay ner)
Town of Wehlen in Germany.

Sonnenuhr (so´ nen er)
Vineyard in Germany literally meaing "sundial"—there's a big sundial in this vineyard.

Kabinett (cab in ett´)
Sweetness level of grapes picked first—producing drier and less sweet German wines.

Qualitatswein Mit Pradikat
(kwal i tahts´ wine mit pre di´ cot)
Abbreviated Q.M.P. means a quality wine with special attributes—the special attributes are the wealth of information on the lable as to the origin (town and vineyard and the sweetness level at which the grapes were picked) of a German wine.

Barossa Valley (bah row´ sa)
Large winemaking region in Australia.

Rioja (ree owe´ ha)
Spanish red wine—one of the best.

Crianza (cree ahn´ za)
Style of making Spanish Rioja in which the wine is aged one year in oak and two years in the bottle before being released.

Reservas (re zer´ vah)
Style of making Spanish Rioja in which the wine is aged one year in oak and two years in the bottle before being released.

Gran Reserva (gran ree zer´ va)
Most expensive way to make a Spanish Rioja. The wine is aged two years in oak, and three years in the bottle before it is released.

PART FOUR

How a Bottle of Wine Gets Its Name

In California, the grape variety in the bottle usually lends its name to the bottle of wine. A wine made up of 75% or more of Cabernet Sauvignon will say "Cabernet Sauvignon" on the label. If Chardonnay makes up 75% or more, it will say "Chardonnay." So on and so forth. A wine, by law, must have at least 75% of one variety to have the name of that variety on the label. This is why a wine, labeled "Cabernet" or "Chardonnay" is said to be a "varietal." The remaining 25% of the mix can be anything the winemaker wants. He may add merlot to his Cabernet to soften it, or a Cabernet Franc to make it fruitier. If a wine does not contain at least 75% of any one variety, but is a blend of whatever the winemaker decides, then he'll give it a generic name like "Estate Blend" or just put the brand name on the label and put "red dinner wine" or just "red wine" on the label. These wines are usually less expensive.

If a winemaker makes a deliberate attempt to fashion his wines like those of Bordeaux, and use the five grape varieties allowed to make these famous French reds, then he will call his wine a meritage (pronounced like heritage) which is the blending of Cabernet Sauvignon, Cabernet Franc, Merlot, Petite Verdot, and Malbec. Wines such as these are usually in blends with no wine having more than 75% of a single variety. These meritages are usually very profound wines with outstanding layering of fruit, due to the blending of the many grape varieties.

In France, a bottle of wine takes its name from the region from where it came. There are five major regions; they are: Burgundy, Bordeaux, Champagne, Rhone Valley, and Loire Valley. Each of these regions is specifically regulated as to what grape varieties to grow, and the amount of grapes that must be harvested per acre. In France, as in California, pruning of the newly formed grape clusters in the spring cuts yields down from 5 or 6 tons per acre, to about 2 or 3 tons per acre. The greatly reduced yield allows all the compounds and nutrients the roots forage for to be concentrated in a smaller amount of grapes—thus greatly intensifying their flavor and character. In general, the more grapes per acre, the less rich and intense the wine will be.

In Burgundy, the predominant and best grape variety for white wine is Chardonnay. The predominant and best red grape in Burgundy is Pinot Noir—unless they come from the village of Beaujolais, and then the Gamay grape is used.

In the Bordeaux region, if you are making red wine, you are allowed to use the following five varieties in any combination, they are: Cabernet Sauvignon, Cabernet Franc, Merlot, Petite Verdot, and Malbec. If you are making white wine in Bordeaux, whether dry or the famous sweet wines of Sauternes—then Sauvignon Blanc and Semillon are used.

In the Champagne region, the two grapes of Burgundy are used, they are of course, Pinot Noir and Chardonnay.

In the Loire Valley, the main grape varieties for white wine are Sauvignon Blanc, Chenin Blanc, Muscadet, and for red wine, Chinon.

In the Rhone Valley, red wines are made predominantly from Syrah, Cinsault, Mouvedre and Grenache. White wines from Rhone are made from Marsanne, and Rousanne.

CONSUMER TIP

If you like a softer red wine, try a merlot, a Beaujolais, or an inexpensive Rioja from Spain.

- Intense red wines are Barolo, Barbaresco, Cabernet Sauvignon, red Bordeaux.

- Sweeter whites include Muscats, Asti Spumante, Chenin Blancs, and some Rieslings.

- Best dry whites are Chardonnay, Sauvignon Blanc, Pinot Grigio, Gavi, and White Rioja.

- Best dessert wines: Sauternes, Barsac, German beerenauslese, trockenbeerenauslese, Eiswein, and from California, try any of the late harvest wines.

At this point you are no doubt wandering why wines labeled "burgundy" and "chablis" or the like end up in gallon jugs, and sell for such astronomically low prices. These are simply California blends of grapes given a French name for the sake of recognition. Remember, French rules are strict in France—but they do not apply to the United States! Are these wines any good? Quality may range from good to bad, depending on the brand, but true varietals are of much better quality, and usually don't come in 4 liter jugs.

In Italy, both grape varieties and regions lend their name to the wines.

The major red grape varieties are Sangiovese, Nebbiolo, and Barbera. Different regions use a specific grape variety, and there are even regions within regions that are very specific, and make outstanding wine.

First, and probably most common is Chianti. Sangiovese is the predominant grape, and the wine must be made in the approved D.O.C. region of Tuscany to say "Chianti" on the label. If a wine is made out of Sangiovese but is not made in Tuscany, it can not say "Chianti"; it will say simply "Sangiovese". Two smaller subregions in Tuscany making wines out of Sangiovese are Montalcino and Montepulciano. It may take years of aging before the tannins are soft enough for consumption. These wines are called Brunello di Montalcino and Vino Nobile di Montepulciano.

Nebbiolo makes profound and immense red wines. They are some of the most intense red wines in the world. These wines are from the region called Piedmont. The wines are: Barolo, Barbaresco, and Gattinara.

Barbaresco is the least intense of the wines, aging two years before it is released, but able to be aged for 15 to 20 years. Barolo is aged for 36 months before being released, and is usually a tannic monster. It will age for 25 to 30 years. My God.

Valpolicella and Bardolino are villages producing soft red wines. These villages also give their name to the wine. Barbera is a wine made from the Barbera grape. It makes very good red wines of medium body. Lambrusco gives its name to the light, slightly sparkling, red wine. Italian white wines are light and simple and are no where near the quality or intensity of the reds.

White wines are Pinot Grigio, Trebbiano—both take their names from the grape variety. Another Italian white wine is the very popular Asti Spumante. Made in the town of Asti, Italy, and from the grape variety called Muscat; this wine is the White Zinfandel of Italy. Light and easy to drink, yet it is slightly sweet and very inoffensive.

The grape variety Malvasia makes a good dry or sweet white wine, usually of the same name.

In Germany, a bottle of wine gets its name from the town and vineyard in which the grapes were grown, followed by the grape variety (Riesling or one of its hybrids are the only grapes allowed) and then, the sweetness level at which the grapes were picked. For example, a Piesporter Goldtropfchen Riesling Spatlese tells you that this wine came from the town of

Piesport, the Goldtropfchen vineyard, made from the Riesling grape, and picked at the second level of sweetness, Spatlese. A Wehlener Sonnenuhr Riesling Kabinett comes from the town of Wehlen, the sonnenuhr ("sonnenuhr" means sundial—there is a big sundial in this vineyard) vineyard, the Riesling grape variety, and the Kabinett sweetness level.

When a German wine gives all of this information, it is said to be a Q.M.P.—or, a Qualitatswein Mit Pradikat—a quality wine with special attributes. All German wines will have at least a "Q" on the label—meaning they are a quality wine, but a Q.M.P. is the highest designation a German wine can have. This wine will only come from this town, only from this village, only this grape, and only this sweetness level.

Also on a German label will be the vintage date. This is the year in which the grapes were harvested. This will give you information about the wine, since the climate in which the grapes were grown, and the specific growing conditions of that year, will make the wine have very special qualities.

Other countries use a combination of the French region style, and the California grape variety style to name a bottle of wine. Both Chili and Australia use grape varieties, but Australia might also say "Barossa Valley", to let the consumer know that it is from a very good wine producing region. There are some interesting blends coming from South Africa, and these wines are either known by the producer or a copyrighted brand name.

In Spain, the major red wine is called Rioja, and is made in three different styles. Crianza is aged at least 12 months in oak before being released, and is the least expensive.

Next is Reservas, aged a year in oak and two years in the bottle before being released and is more expensive; most expensive is Gran Reservas, aged two years in oak, and three years in the bottle. These are the most expensive. You will see one of these designations on the bottle along with "Rioja" in big letters. The name of the producer will also be supplied. Spanish white wines, like Italian white wines, are simple, straight forward, inexpensive quaffing white wines.

REVIEW AND REITERATION
PART FOUR

- In California, a bottle of wine takes its name from the grape variety. Cabernet Sauvignon, Merlot, Chardonnay, etc., are all names of grapes, and, the name of the wine if at least 75% of that grape variety comprises the wine in the bottle. This, then, is called a varietal wine—having at least 75% of that variety of grape making up the wine.

- In France, the region lends its name to the bottle of wine, and each region is strictly regulated as to what grape it can produce, and even how many grapes per ton can be harvested. Major grape growing regions are: Burgundy, Bordeaux, Rhone Valley, Loire Valley, and Champagne.

- Pinot Noir and Chardonnay are the major grapes in the Burgundy region. Pinot Noir makes red wines, and Chardonnay the white wines.

- Cabernet and Merlot make the majority of red wines in Bordeaux, France, and in making the white wines in Bordeaux, Sauvignon Blanc and Semillon are used.

- In the Rhone Valley, France, Syrah, Cinsault, and Mouvedre make the red wines, while Marsanne and Rousanne make up the white wines.

- Pinot Noir and Chardonnay are the two grapes allowed to make Champagne in the region Champagne, France.

- In the Loire Valley, Sauvignon Blanc and Chenin Blanc make up the white wines—these are Sancere and Vouvray respectively. Muscadet also makes a pleasing white—called simply Muscadet. Chinon makes a pleasant red wine.

- In Italy, both the grape varieties and the region can give their names to the bottle of wine.

- Chianti is made predominantly from the grape variety called Sangiovese, and Chianti must be made in Tuscany—or it can not be called Chianti. Brunello di Montalcino and Vino Nobile di Montepulciano are both made from the grape Sangiovese, and each in the subdivisions of Tuscany called Moltalcino and Montepulciano. Wines made from Sangiovese, but not from Tuscany are usually called "Sangiovese."

- In the Piedmont region of Italy, the grape variety Nebbiolo makes the intense reds, specifically Barolo, and Barbaresco—each specific towns in the Piedmont region.

- In Asti, Italy, a light sparkling wine made from the Muscat grape makes Asti Spumante.

REVIEW AND REITERATION
PART FOUR

■ In Germany, the best wines are labeled Qualitatswein Mit Pradikat—Quality wines with special attributes. On these bottles, the name of the town, followed by the vineyard, the grape variety, and then the sweetness level will be on the front of the bottle.

■ Countries such as Chili and Australia usually use the grape varieties to name a bottle of wine.

■ In Spain, Riojas are the most popular table wine, and the ever popular Sherry has been pleasuring people for centuries.

PART FIVE

How to Read a Wine Label

PRONUNCIATION GUIDE
PART FIVE

Auslese (ahs´ lay say)
Means "outpicked"—Germany uses this term to describe the late harvest grapes picked out of, or after, harvesting of the grapes used to make less sweet wines. These grapes are much sweeter.

Beerenauslese (ba´ ron ahs lay say)
Literally, the individually picked berries ("beeren") of the outpicked wine—only the ripest are used.

Trockenbeerenauslese
(tro´ ken ba ron ahs lay say)
Literally, the driest (therefore the sweetest) of the individually picked ripest berries, of the outpicked wine.

Eiswein (iesh´ vine)
Beerenauslese sweetness level of grapes that are frozen when temps drop to 25 degrees. Grapes are hurriedly picked and all ice removed. Only sugar and must remain. Sweet German dessert wine able to age for decades.

Botrytis Cinerea (bow try´ tis sin er ee´ ah)
The noble rot, a fungus that develops on grapes. When formed at the right time, on the right grapes, makes superb dessert wines. If it forms at the wrong time, on the wrong grape, the grapes just rot, and are unusable.

Mosel (moe´ zel)
German river. Grapes are planted on its steep banks, and make superb wine.

Saar (sar)
Tributary of the Mosel river.

Ruwer (roor)
Tributary of the Mosel river.

Rhein (rine)
Great River running through Germany. Vineyards are planted on the banks and in the inland areas of this river. The wines are outstanding.

Chateau (sha toe´)
French for house or castle. Bordeaux bottles have this designation, and it means that grapes in this bottle of wine were grown and fermented on this property, if and only if it also says,"mis en bouteille au chateau," or produced and bottled at this chateau.

Mis en bouteille au chateau
(mice en bow tee ah sha toe)
Bottled at this chateau. Bordeaux wines will say this when the grapes are grown and bottled at the chateau whose name appears on the label.

Lafite Rothschild (la feet´ roth shield)
One of the five first growth wine properties.

Mouton Rothschild (moo tawn roth shield)
One of the five first growth wine properties.

Margaux (mar go´)
One of the five first growth properties.

Latour (la tour´)
One of the five first growth properties.

Haut-Brion (owe bree own´)
One of the five first growth properties.

St. Estephe (es tef´)
Great winemaking region of Bordeaux.

Pauillac (poo ee ak´)
Great winemaking region of Bordeaux.

St. Julian (jew lee en´)
Great winemaking region of Bordeaux.

Pomerol (paw mer all´)
Great winemaking region of Bordeaux.

St. Emilion (a mee lee en´)
Great winemaking region of Bordeaux.

Puligny-Montrachet
(poo lee nee   mah ra shay)
Great winemaking town of Burgundy in which half of the 19 acre Montrachet vineyard exists.

Chasagne Montrachet
(sha shanya mah ray shay)
Great winemaking town that encompasses about half of the Montrachet vineyard.

Batard Montrachet (ba tar´)
One of the great Montrachet winemaking vineyards.

Chevalier Montrachet (shev el yay)
One of the great winemaking vineyards of Montrachet.

PART FIVE

Chablis (sha blee´)
Great winemaking district southeast of Paris, France.

Grand Cru (graw croo)
Burgundy's finest designation for its best wines.

Premier Cru (pree meer croo)
Burgundy's second best designation for its outstanding wines.

Pommard (pa mar´)
Commune in Burgundy that makes outstanding wine.

Beaune (bone)
Principal center of the Burgundy wine trade.

Nuits-Saint Georges (nwee´ san zhorzh´)
Burgundy region making outstanding red wines. Some whites are also made here.

Chambolle Musigny
(sham bol moo see nee)
Great winemaking town of Burgundy.

Richebourg (reesh´ borg)
One of the great winemaking vineyards in Burgundy—about 20 acres.

Musigny (moo see nee)
One of the greatest winemaking vineyards of Burgundy—about 25 acres.

Bonnes Mares (bone mar)
One of the great winemaking vineyards of Burgundy—about 39 acres.

Pommard Epenots (pa mar´ ep en oh´)
Producer or town (Pommard) stating that this wine is made exclusively from grapes of the Epenots vineyard. Mark of a classic or superlative wine.

Beaune Greves (bone gra vay´)
Town or producer (Beaune), and the specific vineyard, Greves, from which the wine was made. Mark of outstanding quality.

Meursault Perrieres (mair soo pair ee ay´)
Producer or town (Meursault) listing the specific vineyard, Perrieres, from which the wine was made.The mark of a superlative wine.

Carbonic Maceration
(car bon ic mass er ay shun)
Process of making wine in which the juice is fermented inside the whole grape, and then gently pushed or squeezed out. Process which Beaujolais is made; makes exceedingly soft, but not ageworthy wines, since little tannin is obtained from the uncut grape skins.

Beaujolais Villages (bow ja lay´ vi lahj´)
Specific origin of wine stating that the villages that produced the wine had stricter viticultural requirements for their vineyard, and therefore, make better wine than regular "Beaujolais"—which can come anywhere from that area.

Fleurie (flo ree´)
One of the ten top wine producing villages of Beaujolais.

Chiroubles (sher owe´ blay)
One of the ten top wine producing villages of Beaujolais.

Chenas (sha nas´)
One of the ten top wine producing villages of Beaujolais.

Brouilly (broy´ ee)
One of the ten top producing wine villages of Beaujolais.

Julienas (jew lee an´ as)
One of the ten top producing wine villages of Beaujolais.

Morgon (more gon´)
One of the ten top producing wine villages of Beaujolais.

St. Amour (a more´)
One of the ten top producing wine villages of Beaujolais.

Regnie (ren yay´)
One of the ten top producing wine villages of Beaujolais.

Moulin-a-vent (moo law ah vah)
One of the ten top producing wine villages of Beaujolais.

Coute-de-Brouilly (co ta day broy´ ee)
One of the ten top producing wine villages of Beaujolais.

PART FIVE

How To Read A Wine Label

California

Biggest, usually, on the label will be the brand name—either that of the owner or something she has picked out. For example, Ironstone, Martin Bros., Lolonis, etc. The second item on the label, and the second biggest, will be the grape variety, if there is at least 75% of that grape in the wine. If it is a blend, or a meritage, it might say just "red dinner wine," or "meritage" and give the percentage of each of the grapes that went into making up this wine. Meritage is usually a more expensive wine. Red wines labeled only "red wine" are usually inexpensive, but there are exceptions.

By law, a wine has to have at least 75% of the grape variety in the bottle, if its name is to appear on the label, for example, Cabernet Sauvignon, Merlot, Zinfandel, etc. Sometimes the wine will contain specially grown grapes that have been planted and pruned so that the yield is less per acre, and these grapes may also be from a single vineyard where the winemaker feels the grapes of the greatest character are obtained. In this instance, he will also give the name of the vineyard.

There is a winemaker in California whose vineyard contains three distinct types of soil—each producing grapes with a different character. The winemaker calls each of his bottlings by the name of the soils—Red Rock Terrace, Volcanic Hill, and Gravelly Meadow-each of these distinct soil types yields a wine with different characteristics. These "Estate Grown" grapes can be tended and cared for at the owner/winemaker's whim; he can prune much of the fruit off at bud and make highly concentrated wine, or let everything grow and make more wine and charge less, choosing volume over quality.

If the grapes were bought, there is little a winemaker can do to change the character of the grapes. Sometimes a winemaker will have a contract with a grower who will provide him with grapes from a specific vineyard, or a specific area in the vineyard. In this case, the winemaker will give the name of the vineyard, and sometimes the name of the grower. But, in any case, the more extensive and specific the origin of the grapes, the better—

and usually more expensive—the wine will be.

The amount of grapes that the winemaker or grower harvests per acre is directly proportional to the quality of wine. Some of the old vineyards—labeled "Old Vines"—bear very little grapes, sometimes as little as 1/2 ton per acre, compared to the 5 or 6 tons a grower may produce. These grapes, which are very sparsely set on old vines are usually intense in character, and yield wine that is of outstanding flavor and richness. The only problem is that the winemaker can only make a limited amount of wine. This usually severely straps him financially, and he is forced to rip out the old vineyard and plant new vines which will yield a crop that will allow him a cashflow to stay in business. Winemaking is an interesting phenomenon.

The vintage date will also be on the label. This will tell you the date the grapes were harvested—not bottled. The year in which the grapes were harvested will give you specific information about the wine. If it was a cool year, if it was a rainy year, if it was a hot and droughty year, all make different wine. We'll talk more about years in a later chapter. The alcohol content will also be on the label. This is law.

Germany

Germany has perhaps the most user–friendly label in existence. Germany has very strict purity and regulatory laws, and the punishment for what may seem inconsequential to us, may result in long prison terms for the Germans. They are deadly serious about the wines. German wines with a big "Q" on them, or the designation "Qualitatswein" means that the wine is of the highest quality, like all German wines, and that the wine is from a designated region. If a German bottle has Q.M.P. on the label—Qualitatswein Mit Pradikat—then the wine will be from only the town and vineyard that is specified on the label. "Piesporter Goldtropfchen" means that the wine is from the town of Piesport, the Goldtropfchen vineyard. The grape variety is stated next on the label, "Riesling"; sometimes it is left out. The Q.M.P. wines will next state the level of sweetness at the time the grapes were picked.

Kabinett being picked first and is the least sweet; spatlese being picked next and slightly sweeter. Auslese means "out picked", or picked out of, or after harvest. These grapes have more concentrated sugars and a lesser amount of water and make sweet wines. Beerenauslese is a designation that means the best and sweetest berries (German for berries, "Beeren") are picked out of the "out picked" or auslese wines, and, trockenbeerenauslese is a designation that describes picking the driest (trocken) of the berries of the outpicked wine. The driest berries will have the most amount of sugar, and the least amount of water, making them extremely sweet.

Eiswein is made when grapes of the beerenauslese sweetness level are allowed to hang on the vine until a fungus called Botrytis Cinerea forms on them causing even the small amount of water in these grapes to dissipate into the fungus, and the fungus in turn leaves a delicious honey-apricot-lime flavor. The conditions must be exactly right for the fungus to form, and they may only do so once or twice in a decade under the extremely narrow window of opportunity.

Then, the temperature must be about 25 degrees at night, and the grapes are picked, by hand, at 4:00 a.m., before the sun thaws the grapes. The grapes are rushed to machines that mechanically remove all the ice— removing every last speck of water! All that is left is sugar and must. These wines are extravagantly sweet and will last for 25 to 50 years or longer!-- The sugar and alcohol being natural preservatives.

The color of German bottles is also user-friendly, and denote from which region the wine comes from. Green bottles tell that the wine comes from the river region—the Mosel river and its tributaries the Saar and the Ruwer. People will often refer to these as "Mosels." Brown bottles come from the Rhein region and are referred to as "Rheins"—Rheins are a little rounder, and softer. Mosels tend to be racy, crisp, and snappy. Blue bottles are from the Nahe region. These wines are usually very inexpensive and quite easy to drink.

French wine bottles

The five major regions of France: Bordeaux, Burgundy, Champagne, Rhone Valley and Loire Valley, each give the consumer specific information about the origin of the wine, and the more specific the information, the better, and more expensive the wine will be. In the Bordeaux region, the bottle is shaped differently from the Burgundy region. Bordeaux bottles look more like medicine bottles of long ago. The shoulders flare out rather quickly—Burgundy bottles have shoulders which slope very gradually, almost as if the shoulders just gradually expand to envelop the bottle.

Bordeaux bottles will say "Chateau" and then give the name of this chateau. So many winemakers long ago had castles—which is what chateau means—that bordered their vineyards that this "chateau" designation became a Bordeaux trademark. Now, by French law, a chateau can be any house or building that makes wine from the property on which it stands. So, when you see the phrase "mise en bouteille au chateau", or "bottled at this chateau," you can be assured that the grapes were grown here—not purchased—and that the specific vineyard practices that make this wine unique were assiduously adhered to.

Now, these Chateaux (plural of Chateau) have been making wine for a long time, and they have a reputation. The wineries or chateaux that have made the best wine for the longest time are given first growth status. This is the very best classification. There are five Chateaux that have first growth classification. They are: Chateau Lafite Rothschild, Chateau Mouton Rothschild, (a cousin) Chateau Latour, Chateau Margaux, and Chateau Haut-Brion (pronounced "owe-bree own").

Next are the second growths, then third growths, fourth growths and fifth growths. In a given year, a third growth may make a better wine than a first growth, or a fifth growth may make a better wine than a second growth, but overall, the higher the ranking, the better, and once again—the more expensive the wine.

Also on the bottle will be the name of the region. This tells you where specifically in Bordeaux the grapes were made into wine. These regions are: St. Estephe, Pauillac, St. Julien, Pomerol, St. Emilion, Sauternes and Barsac. Sauternes and Barsac are sweet white wines made in Bordeaux. These regions each have different soils, and each make wine that has a different combination of the grapes allowed to make wine in Bordeaux. For red wine these five varieties, Cabernet Sauvignon, Merlot, Cabernet Franc, Petite Verdot and Malbec, may be used in any combination, or are bottled 100% varietal—100% of that grape variety. It will not state this on the label as in California, however, for each year the winemaker may change his formula, so that his final blend reflects the taste he is trying to achieve.

Red Bordeaux usually has a deeper more intense flavor of earth than its California counterpart, although this is a generalization, since many outstanding California wines can be just as intense if not moreso than a great Bordeaux. The flavors of blackberries, and tobacco, and chocolate and leather, permeate the wine. This may sound like an atrocious cacophony of flavors to the beginner, but allowed to mature and age, these nuances make great Red Bordeaux quite profound.

White Bordeaux bottles are shaped the same way as Red Bordeaux bottles. The same information is also included on them. White Bordeaux, at least the dry ones, don't usually bring the very high prices that the red ones do. White Bordeaux are blends of two grapes, and they are Sauvignon Blanc, and Semillon. These wines usually run about 10 to 20 dollars a bottle. The sweet white wines from the regions in Sauternes and Barsac are some of the best wines the world has to offer. Their prices can be staggering, but the quality is exceptional.

What makes these wines so priceless is a tendency for a fungus called Botrytis Cinerea to form on both Semillon and, to a lesser extent, Sauvignon Blanc. As stated previously, this fungus saps all the remaining water from the grape, and in return leaves a honey-apricot and lime flavor. This, in addition to the peaches and guava you normally taste in these wines, makes for a monumentally rich and delicious dessert wine.

Picking these fungus-infected grapes is very time consuming. Each grape must be picked one at a time, and the winemakers divide the lots from the ones they picked in the morning, from the ones they picked in the afternoon; each will have different characteristics, and levels of sugar, acid, and ripeness, and will be blended later for the taste the winemaker is after.

There is a very small window of opportunity that the winemaker must work with if he wants to make a great dessert wine. Only once or twice in a decade are conditions perfect for making outstanding wines. For example, if the fungus forms too early, the grapes will simply rot, or, if the temperature does not allow the fungus to properly mature before the grapes are picked, the flavors will not be intense. There are a myriad of conditions—both climactic and botanical—that must be present. And, if all these conditions are not present? The winemaker will either sell off his grapes, or, produce a wine under another label for less money so that he does not get a bad reputation. Sauternes are sometimes sold in half bottles—because of their concentration, you don't need to drink as much—and to keep them affordable. California also makes excellent dessert wines which can be substituted for Sauternes.

Wine bottles from the Burgundy region are shaped differently from those of Bordeaux. Burgundy bottles have lower sloped shoulders—almost as if the neck of the bottle slowly increases as it descends to the bottom. The label will give you the name of the town, and in more expensive bottles, the name of the vineyard. Sometimes specific rows in the vineyard will even have names! All these very specific items of information tell you that the wine is outstanding in quality, and expensive.

Some examples. There is a vineyard in Burgundy called Montrachet that makes superb white wines. This 19 acre vineyard is situated in two towns. These two towns are called Puligny-Montrachet and Chasagne Montrachet, and take the "Montrachet" part of their name from this vineyard which makes them famous. Also, in the vineyard of Montrachet, there are special sections which are named, these sections are Batard Montrachet, and Chevalier Montrachet. These sections make very little, very outstanding, and very expensive white wine!

The wines that are made from the part of the vineyard that is in the town of Puligny Montrachet is called, simply enough, "Puligny Montrachet." The wine that is made from the town that contains the other half of the Montrachet vineyard, Chasagne Montrachet is called "Chasagne Montrachet". If the wine comes from the special sections of either Batard or Chevalier, it will say Batard Montrachet or Chevalier Montrachet. The Chardonnay grape must be used here. The name Montrachet means bald hill. Because of the very rocky and stony soil, nothing else grows on these slopes except the grapes that are planted, and some scrubby underbush. The grape vines are stressed because of the lack of water and must go in search of food. The roots of the vines are extensive, and the compounds and elements picked up and deposited in the grapes is highly concentrated because there are fewer grapes, and, because there is little water to dilute them.

Another area in Burgundy known for making outstanding wines is

> **CONSUMER TIP**
>
> California labels are usually rather easy to read—stating the grape variety and then the brand or winery. French wine labels are a bit trickier, but once you get used to what to look for, they become familiar.
>
> Ask questions of your local wine merchant. People appreciate such questions and are always glad to share their knowledge with others—especially ones that spend money with them! Note your favorite grape varieties, and brands.

called Chablis. Chablis is a little town southeast of Paris. The surrounding communes and towns make wine that, like both Puligny-Montrachet and Chasagne-Montrachet, must be from the Chardonnay grape. As with other Burgundy wines, the best of the wines from the Chablis region are called Grand Cru—and you will see this designation on the label. The Grand Cru from Chablis will also have the name of the specific vineyard where the grapes were grown. These vineyards are: Vaudesin, Les Clos, Grenouilles, Preuses, Bougros, Valmur, and Blanchots. When you see "Grand Cru" and one of these vineyards, you are getting the best Chablis has to offer.

The second highest level of excellence in Burgundy are wines marked with the designation "Premier Cru". In great years, both Grand Cru, and Premier Cru can be outstanding, but Grand Crus are usually always outstanding. If the label simply says "Chablis"—then it comes from any of the 1600 acres of vineyards in Chablis. These wines are in no way connected to the wines marked "chablis" at the corner grocery store that sell for under 10 dollars a bottle; these simple grocery store wines are mixtures of whatever the winemaker has left over, and usually a little sweet. They use the name because it lends recognition to the wine. Also, France has no jurisdiction in the U.S. to make them stop.

Red Wine from the Burgundy region is also of the highest quality. Names of communes, villages and vineyards all signify outstanding quality. Names of communes like Pommard, Beaune, Nuits-Saint George, Chambolle Musigny, are signs that the wine is highly regulated, comes from that town, and that there is a very limited supply. Again, as in areas which make White Burgundy, specific vineyard plots in areas which make red Burgundy are signs of the utmost quality, and price. Names of specific sections of vineyards, such as Richebourg, Musigny, Bonnes Mares, make precious little wine, and the prices reflect this. Often, the label will state both the vineyard, and the producer, such as Pommard Epenots, Beaune Creves, Mearsalt Perrieres, etc. Pinot Noir is the grape variety which makes all the best wines from these vineyards in Burgundy. In fact, no other grape may be used here.

There is a town in southern Burgundy called Beaujolais which makes some very special red wines. These are the famous "nouveau" or new wines of the year. They are made from a grape called Gamay, are crushed in October, and the wine is released and ready to be consumed on the third

Thursday in November! These light and fruity red wines are made from a process called carbonic maceration. These grapes are put in huge tanks—the whole grape, they are not crushed as in other red wines—and the weight of the grapes cracks them open, allowing the wild yeasts to enter and ferment the wine inside the whole grape. The free-run juice is then gently pushed out. The resulting wine is very fruity and very soft. It is not very ageworthy since there is not enough tannin to allow it to age. Beaujolais should be consumed in the first year of its release.

If a wine comes from anywhere in Beaujolais, and from no town or distinct vineyard, the label will say just "Beaujolais." Now, as in other French wines, as the information gets more specific, the wines are of higher quality, and they are sometimes more expensive. If a wine says "Beaujolais Villages," it comes from the thirty some villages who have more stringent viticultural practices, and more work intensive winemaking procedures, such as a specific tonnage of grapes per acre, which would entail more pruning, different types of trellising, etc. If the Beaujolais comes from the ten or so villages who have their own name on the label, the wine is the highest quality of all. Each of these villages say that the wine that comes from their village, and their vineyard, has its own unique flavor. Although there is some slight variation, it would be difficult for the average person to distinguish between them.

These villages are: Fleurie, Chiroubles, Chenas, Brouilly, Julienas, Morgon, St. Amour, Regnie, Moulin-a-Vent, and Coute-de-Brouilly. I said "ten or so" even though there are currently ten villages putting their individual names on the label because at anytime, a village from the wines marked "Beaujolais Village" may submit to the more stringent requirements for them to put their individual name on the label. Regnie is the latest to do this, before, being just one of the villages who combined their grapes with the others for "Beaujolais Village."

In Italy, white wines will usually have either the name of the grape variety on the label, or the name of the region from which it came. The same information applies to red wine. White wines labeled "Trebbiano" and "Pinot Grigio" are simply of these grape varieties. White wines like "Gavi" come from the region in Piedmont called "Gavi" and are made from the grape called Cortese. "Asti" comes from the town of Asti, is made from the grape called Muscat, and is slightly sparkling.

Red wines labeled Gattinara, Barola, and Barbaresco, are made from the grape called Nebbiolo, and are in the Piedmont region. Chianti and Brunello are from Tuscany and are made from the grape variety Sangiovese. Vintage dates—the date the grapes were harvested—are on the label, along with the alcohol content, and sometimes the proprietor's name. Some of the best of the Italian winemakers are venturing out on their own, and making wines that are not of the grape variety permitted in a specific region. Some of these wines, like those of Angelo Gaja, are some of the best Italy has to offer, but can not list a specific classification like D.O.C.G. (Denominazione di Origine Controllata e Garantita) which guarantees the strictest and the best winemaking procedures in Italy.

Gaja does not use the grapes of the region, nor does he submit his wine for the classification. Few, if any, would argue the exceptional quality and care that go into Gaja's wines. And the missing (D.O.C.G.) classification in this case, means little. Gaja uses Cabernet Sauvignon for his red wines, and Chardonnay for his whites—these are also the great grapes of California, and France. His wines are perhaps, some of the best the world has to offer. Other countries use a combination of grape varieties and regions on their labels, in addition to the vintage date, and the alcohol content.

Some countries guarantee that the wine in the bottle actually comes from the place where the label says it does. In France, the A.O.C., or, Appellation d´ Origine Controlee guarantees place, grape varieties, and winemaking procedures. In Italy, D.O.C., or Denominazione di Origine Controllata means that the wine is made in specific areas using specific techniques. D.O.C.G., or Denominazione di Origine Controllata e Garantita, is used for higher status wines, and guarantees place and name.

REVIEW AND REITERATION
PART FIVE

■ In California, a bottle of wine takes its name from the grape variety. Cabernet Sauvignon, Merlot, Chardonnay, etc., are all names of grapes, and, the name of the wine if at least 75% of that grape variety comprises the wine in the bottle. This, then, is called a varietal wine— having at least 75% of that variety of grape making up the wine.

■ California wine labels usually have the name of the winery, or the owners last name in the biggest letters. If the wine contains at least 75% of one grape variety, it will have this name, somewhere very prominent on the front. Cabernet Sauvignon, Chardonnay and Riesling are examples. This wine is called a varietal: at least 75% of one variety. Also on the label will be the year the grapes were harvested— the vintage date—and, the alcohol level.

■ California wines with less than 75% of any variety are just labeled "red wine" or "white wine". If the blend is a mixture of grapes used to make Bordeaux wines—either red or white—then this wine is called a meritage. Meritage is more expensive than a "red" or "white" wine, usually.

■ California wines which name specific vineyards or specific soil types usually have unique characteristics for which the vintner is proud, and therefore will put these names on the label also.

■ In Germany, wines marked with "Q" or "Q.B.A." means "a quality wine of a designated region." The "Q" stands for "Qualitatswein" or, quality wine. The German wines marked "Q.M.P."—quality wine with special attributes—always give the name of the town, the vineyard, the grape variety, and then the sweetness level. Generally, Kabinett is ever so slightly sweet, spatlese is sweeter, auslese very sweet, beerenauslese and trockenbeerenauslese are extremely sweet. Eiswein is the must and sugar of frozen grapes in which all the water has been mechanically removed as ice. They are very rich and sweet.

■ German wine bottles are also very user-friendly. Brown bottles signify the wine is from the Rhein region—or inland—these wines are softer and rounder. Green bottles signify the wine is from vineyards bordering the Mosel river or its tributaries the Saar and the Ruwer. Blue bottles tell us the wine is from the Nahe region.

■ French wine bottles are shaped differently from region to region.

■ Burgundy bottles have very low sloped shoulders—almost as if the neck just slowly descends to encompass the bottle.

REVIEW AND REITERATION
PART FIVE

■ Bordeaux bottles look like medicine bottles of long ago—very high prominent shoulders.

■ "Chateau" is a Bordeaux trademark and the phrase "mis en bouteille au chateau" means that the wines have been produced and bottled by the property—or chateau—given on the front label. The grapes were not purchased; they were raised here, and made into wine here; it is the highest designation of quality.

■ Bordeaux classifies its wines by arranging them into "growth" status. First growth being the best, and fifth growth being the last of the top five—but still very good. Lesser wines are ranked below the five top growths.

■ Dry white wines from the Bordeaux region are good, but the sweet dessert wines of Bordeaux from the regions of Sauternes and Barsac are some of the most magnificent wines in the world. Their prices and their quality are astronomical!

■ White wines from the Burgundy region all have some very specific information on the label, and the more specific, the better the wine.

■ Montrachet is a 19 acre vineyard that lies in two towns—Puligny Montrachet and Chasagne Montrachet. Wines from each town will bear that name. Batard Montrachet and Chevalier Montrachet are specially designated areas in the Montrachet vineyard. These produce very little—but superlative—wines.

■ Chablis is another area of Burgundy. Grand Cru is the highest designation, and will give the name of the vineyard the wine was produced from. Premier Cru is the next best classification of Burgundy, and wines that just say "Chablis" come from anywhere in the 1600 acre vineyard.

■ Both the Montrachet vineyard and the area of Chablis use only the Chardonnay grape to make their wines.

■ Red wines from Burgundy use a grape called Pinot Noir—except the area of Beaujolais—which uses the Gamay grape.

■ Like white wines from this region, the more extensive and specific information given on the label of the red Burgundy, the better the wine will be. Look for specific towns, and producers.

■ Beaujolais is a light red wine consumed only months after harvesting and bottling. Beaujolais "Nouveau"—the new wine—is released on the third Thursday of November. The more specific the information, along with names of villages the wine is from—the better the wine.

PART SIX

The Restaurant Wine List

PART SIX

Sommelier (som el yay´)
Person who usually makes the wine lists and directs the wine operations at a restaurant. Either he, or one of his assistants help patrons make wine selections and help when ordering both food and wine.

Pouilly Fuisse (poo ee fwee say´)
White wine from the Burgundy region which makes excellent dry white wine from the Chardonnay grape.

Salutre (so loo´ tray)
One of the four communes of the Pouilly-Fuisse district.

Fuisse (fwee say´)
One of the four communes of the Pouilly-Fuisse district.

Vergisson (ver´ ja sin)
One of the four communes of the Pouilly-Fuisse district.

Chaintre (shan tray´)
One of the four communes of the Pouilly-Fuisse district.

Macon (may con´)
Important wine making town in southern Burgundy.

Chateau D´ Yquem (dya kem´)
One of the best sweet dessert wines from Sauternes, in Bordeaux.

Chateau Climens (kla menz´)
One of the greatest wines of the Barsac region. Outstanding dessert wine.

Doisy Daene (doy zee dane)
Very good to excellent (classified as a second growth) sweet dessert wine of Barsac region in Sauternes.

Filhot (fee yo)
Excellent dessert wine of the Sauternes region.

Guiraud (ghee row´)
Classified first growth dessert wine of Sauternes.

Rieussec (ree´ owe sec)
First growth status dessert wine of the Sauternes region.

Suduiraut (soo doo´ i row)
First growth status Sauternes.

Tawny port (taw´ nee)
Dark brown-colored port due to oak aging. Usually more expensive than ruby port.

Ruby port (roo´ bee)
Bright red-colored port that has not been aged. Usually less expensive than tawny port.

Jerez (hair eth´)
Spanish city where sherry originated.

Palomino (pal o mee´ no)
Grape from which Sherry is made.

Solera (so lair´ ah)
System of arranged barrels in which older Sherry is fractionally blended with the new Sherry.

Blanc de blanc (blahnc da blahnc)
Literally "white wine from a white grape"—a designation telling you that this Champagne is made from 100% Chardonnay.

Blanc de Noir (blahnc da Nwar)
Designation telling you that Champagne is made from 100% Pinot Noir. Literally "white wine from a black grape."

Methode Chapenoise
(me thode´ cham pen wha´)
Best and most expensive way of making Champagne. In this process, secondary fermentation takes place in the same bottle the wine is sold in.Marked "Fermented in THIS bottle" on the label.

Charmat or Vat method (shar-ma)
Cheapest way to make Champagne in which the secondary fermentation takes place in a vat. The wine is then put in bottles for sale.

Riddling (rid´ ling)
Process by which the bottles in the Methode Champenoise process of making Champagne are slowly turned after secondary fermentation so that dead yeast and sediment end up at the neck of the bottle so it can easily be taken out.

Disgorging (dis gor´ jing)
Process of removing the plug of sediment from riddled bottles.

Dosage' (doe saj´)
Adding a mixture of sugar and wine to the final blend of champagne to achieve a desired level of sweetness or dryness.

Bead (beed)
The grade of the bubbles produced in Champagne. They should be persistent, and fine—making the wine creamy—not gassy as big bubbles would.

PART SIX

The Restaurant Wine List
· ·

Few things are more terrifying than being handed a wine list in a restaurant and having the sommelier or waiter standing there waiting for your selection. A few simple rules, and you'll have no problem whatsoever.

Somewhere on the list will be the infamous "glass pours". These wines "by the glass" are usually the least expensive offered by the restaurant. You may see names here like "Burgundy" or "Chablis" which are euphemisms for a slightly sweet red or white that is soft and easy to drink, but does not have a lot of character and flavor. These glass pours are for customers who do not want to order a whole bottle of wine either because they are by themselves, or, only one person at the table wants to drink wine.

In a few instances, wine friendly restaurants will offer wines "by the glass" from known winemakers, like Fess Parker, or Martin Bros., or Lolonis. These are excellent brand name wines, and although they may cost a buck more a glass than the "glass pours," they are really worth it.

A serious enthusiast of wine would never order a "glass pour" unless it was the only wine there, or, it came from a reputable winemaker. A step up from the glass pours which are simply marked either "red" or "white" or "Burgundy" or "Chablis" is the actual name of the grape. These will actually say "Cabernet" or "Chardonnay," and if the restaurant is actually selling Cabernet and Chardonnay and not using these names as euphemisms for red and white, you are actually slightly above the "Burgundy" or "Chablis" classification.

Ask the waiter or sommelier if these are decent Cabernets and Chardonnays, or if they're junk. He will usually tell you the truth. If you are genuinely serious about your wine, and would like something decent, then order from the wines that are offered by the bottle. If you must order from the "wines by the glass list" then, follow these rules.

For red wines, if you want something dry and red, order a "Burgundy," or a "Cabernet"—the latter, hopefully, will be a Cabernet. If you want a dry white, order the "Chablis" or the "Chardonnay." Sweet, or semi-sweet wines that are white may be under the heading of "Riesling," "Chenin Blanc," "Muscat," or "White Zinfandel." There are no real sweet reds, unless you look at some of the dessert wines. Softer reds may come under the heading of "Beaujolais," "Lambrusco," "Bardolino," or "Valpolicella."

Next on the wine list will be the wines that the restaurant offers by the bottle. If the restaurant has an extensive "cellar"—a place where the wines are kept—then his list will be quite large. Some restaurants are actually rated by the amount of wine they have listed and in their cellars.

Chardonnays will usually be first on the list. Chardonnay is a dry white wine, and when you start to drink a few of the many on the market, you will obviously favor some over the others. Note the names of the brands that you prefer, and when you go to a restaurant, ask the sommelier if he has these brands. If he does not, simply tell him what you liked about this brand, and he will be able to substitute something on his list. If he looks at you like you are from another planet, it's your turn to be impatient and upset—ask him if he knows his wines—and if its "not too much trouble" to suggest something equivalent to your favorite. If he can't, simply ask for a waiter or sommelier who is a little more knowledgeable or helpful.

These people are supposed to be there to help you. Don't tip them if they act like it's a God-given right that they should be tipped whether they help you or not. You work for your money, politely have them work for theirs. Ask; Ask; Ask. Be persistent, and don't let them bully you into either a quick decision, or a choice that they know nothing about.

Prices of the Chardonnays will depend on a few things. Most notable, the vineyard practices where the grapes were grown, and the amount of time spent in oak. More expensive selections spend longer time in expensive oak barrels; they also have more intensive viticultural techniques— such as extensive pruning of the fruit—which curtails the amount of wine made, but really increases the quality of the wine. Oak barrels are usually used only three years or so for great wine, then, these barrels are used by either other wineries for cheaper wines, or, by this winery for a second, less expensive label.

Why? Because all the rich and buttery oak flavors picked up by the wine—and imparted by the barrels—occur in the first few years of use. After this, the oak flavors are greatly reduced. So these barrels—which cost about 600 to 800 dollars for a 60 gallon barrel—can be used only a few times for great wines! No wonder excellent Chardonnay is so expensive! Some of the Chardonnays that are not so expensive on the wine list are the ones aged in "older oak." Much less expensive, much less taste, usually more profitable.

These less expensive Chardonnays usually have fruit that is pruned less—increasing the yields per acre—or are from purchased grapes. These wines are lighter—the industry word for "diluted", but are much more affordable, and most are rather good, but not outstanding.

The restaurant will probably list the Cabernets next. This will probably be followed by Merlots, then Zinfandels, and Pinot Noirs and Syrahs. These are all California red wines. Most intense will be the Cabernet Sauvignons. A small, thick-skinned grape, Cabernets are usually very intense and ageworthy red wines. Remember, Cabernet is the predominant red grape of the Bordeaux region in France, and makes the most intense reds of that region also.

If you are a serious red wine drinker, or, have guests at your table that really enjoy serious red wines, Cabernets are the wines to order. Syrahs and Petite Sirahs can almost be as intense as Cabernets, and are usually good from both California, and Australia. Softer wines include Merlot and Pinot Noir. Merlots are graceful and less tannic than the Cabernets; they are also less ageworthy.

Pinot Noirs make the great Burgundies of France. The wines can be intense in flavor—and yet graceful and soft, or, they can be tannic and austere and harsh and downright lean and mean. In my experience, Pinot Noirs can be extremely good, or extremely bad.

My advice: if you don't know of a brand name that you trust, or, the waiter is not wine knowledgeable and therefore cannot make a suggestion, pass on the Pinots. Fess Parker winery, however, has been making outstanding Pinot Noirs, and you might want to try one, or ask the sommelier if he has any on the list.

Red Zinfandels are a good solid choice for red wines. Lolonis probably makes the best Zinfandels. Martin Brothers also makes some delicious red Zinfandels. Wildhurst is another excellent brand.

Next on the restaurant wine list will be the French wines. Go back and read the chapters on "How To Read A Wine Label" and "How A Bottle Of Wine Gets Its Name" right now. I'll wait...OK.

The Bordeaux red wines will probably be next. Remember, these are just blends of Cabernet Sauvignon, Merlot, Cabernet Franc, Petite Verdot, and Malbec, so they will taste similar to California Cabernets. You will see the word "Chateau" followed by the name of the wine.

The five first growths will be the most expensive, and the older the wine, the more expensive it will probably be—especially if it was a great year. If the price of these wines does not bother you, they are exceptionally good choices. If you need to impress someone who loves red wine, one of the five first growths is the way to do it. These wines are, once again, Chatea Latour, Chateau Mouton Rothschild, Chateau Lafite Rothschild, Chateau Haut-Brion, and Chateau Margaux.

It's difficult to try and explain all the different nuances of wine from all the varying regions, so we can make a generalization that as the wines from Bordeaux get less expensive, they will have spent less time in oak, will have yielded more tons of grapes per acre—so the wine will be less intense, and will generally be less impressive, although good, than the more expensive top growths. There are some good bargains to be found in some of the less expensive Bordeaux. The main thing to remember is that red Bordeaux are like California Cabernets—big, dry, red, wines.

White Bordeaux will follow. These are blends of Semillon and Sauvignon Blanc. They are dry and crisp, and not real intense. White Bordeaux (except the Sauternes) are inexpensive and do not come near the quality of the red wines. If you enjoy an herbal and grassy white wine, you will enjoy White Bordeaux.

The Red Burgundies will be next. These are the great red wines from the Burgundy region in France. They are made out of the grape variety Pinot Noir. They are outstanding in a number of ways. Red Burgundy (Pinot Noir) has a different tannin structure than that of Red Bordeaux (Cabernet Sauvignon). The wines taste softer, even though there is as much tannin as Cabernet, but also age extremely well. The taste of Red Burgundy is also rather different. They have a meaty flavor—almost like that of bacon cooking, with overtunes of cherries—very unique. When they are good, they are like a 150 piece orchestra—the gracious notes of the violins—the cherries—the bass, the bacon, and all the subtle nuances of flavors are like trumpets, and triangles, and cymbals; they are just great!

A bad Pinot Noir, or one that is not well made will be harsh, and acidic, and dry—it will give you the same sensation as the 150 piece orchestra—but instead of in concert—imagine the instruments on a bus, and the bus collided head on with another bus. So, I would suggest that unless you know your Red Burgundy very well, or know a sommelier you trust, Red Burgundies represent a true leap of faith when ordering from a restaurant wine list.

California red wine, and Red Bordeaux offer a much safer selection. If you really insist on a Red Burgundy, look for not only the town, but also a vineyard designation. Names of towns which denote outstanding Red Burgundy are Pommard, Beaune, Nuits-Saint George, Chambolle Musigny. Pommard Epenets, Beaune Creves, Meursalt Perrieres are all towns and their producers. These are outstanding wines.

White Burgundies are as stunning as the Red Burgundies. Unlike White Bordeaux (except Sauternes) which is only good at best, compared to the Red Bordeaux.

Remember the vineyard called Montrachet that we talked about in previous chapters? Look for that name when selecting a good White Burgundy. If it says only "Montrachet" on the label, and gives no further towns or vineyards, it is from the Montrachet vineyard, but anywhere from that vineyard. If the label says "Puligny Montrachet," then it comes from the part of the vineyard that lies in the town of Puligny-Montrachet, and was made by the people in that town. If it says "Chasagne Montrachet," then it comes from the part of the vineyard that lies in the town of Chasagne Montrachet. The same applies for Chablis.

If there is only the designation "Chablis" on the label, it came from any of the 1600 acres in Chablis. If the label has the designation Chablis, and then the name of the vineyard such as Vaudesin, Les Clos, Grenouilles, Valmur, Blanchots, Preuses, ad Bougros, then the label will say "Grand Cru"—these are the best wines Chablis has to offer. Burgundy which has the designation "Premier Cru" is the middle classification—not as specialized as the Grand Cru, but not as pedestrian as the common Burgundy. Also in the White Burgundy section will be the Pouilly Fuisse. I'm sure many of you have heard of this famous French wine. Pouilly Fuisse is made out of the Chardonnay grape, like all white Burgundies, but is usually less expensive. It comes from four small communes in southern Burgundy. These communes are Solutre, Fuisse, Vergisson, and Chaintre. Pouilly Fuisse is very dry and racy. It is best consumed in the first three years of its life.

Meursault will also be listed under White Burgundy, and is made from the Chardonnay grape also. Green-gold in color, Meursault is a little higher in alcohol content, but is superbly balanced. It has the subtle flavor of roasted hazelnuts, and tends to be not as austere as some of the other White Burgundies. It is an excellent wine.

Least expensive of the White Burgundies will be the Macon, or the Macon Villages. These are made predominantly from the Chardonnay grape, but a grape called Aligote is sometimes used. It does not have the class and character of Chardonnay. Macon Villages is a bit higher in quality, because it must come from a designated commune or village. Remember, the more extensive and specific the information, the better the wine will be.

The Italian wines on the wine list can be organized in a number of different ways. We'll discuss the types of wine, and no matter how they are organized, you will be able to understand what is being stated. Italy has some of the most unique and intense red wines in the world. These monster reds have the flavor of leathers, and tar, and tobacco, and chocolate and coffee, and even licorice! Their tastes are some of the most profound you will ever experience.

The wines that fall into this category are from a region called Piedmont. Red wines in the Piedmont region are made from the grape called Nebbiolo, and the wines made from this grape are Barbaresco, Barolo, and Gattinara. Of these three red wines, Barbaresco is the one that is a little bit softer—but it is still a monumental red! Next in intensity is Barolo. Able to last decades after bottling, Barolo, is a red wine-drinker's red wine. Gattinara, made from Nebbiolo grapes, is also a unique red wine.

White wines from this region are the ever popular Asti-Spumante, which is made in the township of Asti in Piedmont, from the Muscat grape. Asti is one of the most popular sparkling white wines both in Italy and the U.S.A. Another white wine popular in the Piedmont region is Gavi. Gavi is made in the town of Gavi and is a dry white wine that is probably Italy's finest.

The Piedmont region, because of the Barbaresco, Barolo, and Gattinara for red wines, and Asti Spumante and Gavi for the whites, is easily Italy's main wine producing region both in quality and quantity.

The second most important region is that of Tuscany. Tuscany uses a grape variety called Sangiovese, and makes the wine all are vastly familiar with—Chianti. Chianti is predominantly Sangiovese which is made in Tuscany. Chianti is medium to light-bodied, has an orange to light red color, and can be a bit tangy at times, sometimes a bit biting, sometimes a bit harsh. The best are the Riservas—they are aged longer, and therefore somewhat mellower.

The regular Chianti Chassicos are aged less, and not as rich as the Chianti Classico Riserva. Brunello di Montalcino and Vino Nobile di Montepulciano are specific regions in Tuscany, and each use the Sangiovese grape also. Brunello is more intense than Chianti, and has more depth and breadth, and breeding. It is a magnificent red—although not as intense as the Barolos and Barbarescos and Gattinaras from Piedmont—but outstanding in quality and ageability. Most of the wine from Tuscany, about 99.9% is red. So with just two regions, Tuscany and Piedmont, we have just about summed up the most important wines of Italy that you will find on a wine list!

Some of the wines you may also see from lesser important regions which produce pleasant, but not important wines are Valpolicella and Bardolino. These light and inexpensive red Italian wines are exported heavily, and no doubt you have seen them. Lambrusco is a light, slightly sparkling red wine and also exported heavily. White wines from Italy, like the white wines of Bordeaux, France, are no where near the quality of their red counterparts, but the Pinot Grigios and Trebbianos are light and simple and crisp and snappy. Pinot Grigio and Trebbiano are the grape varieties, and they also give the bottle of wine its name.

There may also be a section on the wine list that offer wines from Chili and Australia. Australia makes some excellent wines, and if you see names like "Henschke" and "Pennfolds", this is a true mark of quality. These two wineries are at the pinnacle of Australia's winemaking industry. Australia does a superlative job with a grape variety called "Shiraz."

You may also see "Syrah" used interchangeably with Shiraz. It is a big rich red wine that is either bottled by itself, or in blends with Cabernet Sauvignon. Australia's wine is very much in style with that of California—their Chardonnays are usually buttery and rich, and some excellent values will be found here. The reds are big and rich and expansive with good amount of oak. They are very well made. As in California, the grape varieties usually lend their name to a bottle of wine, or, the grower or winery will have their name on the bottle, and underneath their name will be the blend of grapes that make up the wine.

Wines from Chili are good, but few, if any, are outstanding. There are some good values here, but don't look for blockbuster reds from this country. Most of the whites are simple and clean, and inexpensive. The name of the grape varieties used to make the wine will appear on the bottle, as in California.

No serious wine list would be complete without dessert wines. These rich and delicious wines go well all by themselves, or, with any dessert you can imagine or create. The expansive flavor and richness of a dessert wine coupled with just fruit is unbelievably good.

Let's review the process by which all dessert wines are made. This includes Germany, France, and California Late Harvest. Dessert wines are made from grapes picked late in the season. These are called "late harvest" and contain a large amount of sugar, and very little water—thus, they are very sweet. Also, grapes on the vine this late in the year have a tendency to develop a fungus called Botrytis Cinerea—"the noble rot"—which, contrary to what you might think, is not only desirable, but greatly increases the

CONSUMER TIP

When ordering wine from a restaurant wine list, first look over the list so you get an idea of what's in it, and how it is laid out. Most of the information in a restaurant wine list tells you absolutely nothing—especially the descriptions. These descriptions are generally simplified ways of trying to get across to the patron what the wine might taste like—but they don't taste like this anyway.

Most important will be your knowledge of the different grape varieties and the preferences you make while tasting wine or dining out. Try to make mental notes of your preferences—or write them on a slip of paper and store them for when you buy at the retail store. Best of all, use a pocket computer to store bits of wine tasting information.

A sommelier will likely help—they just look intimidating. Most of the ones you will come in contact with will be overjoyed to help you spend your money; the last thing they want to do is alienate a good client. Now, they will have a preference, but don't let their preference overrule yours—unless you want to try something different.

And, most importantly, any wine that you like is appropriate with any food. What might be a great choice for me could be disastrous for you. It is your money, and your decision. Be in charge and drink what you want with the food you're ordering; nobody argues with a person who knows his own mind, and if you have a preference, you know your own mind—now get out there and order something!!!

depth and breadth of flavors present in the wine. Conditions have to be just right for the fungus to form, and if it forms too early, the grapes will just rot and be unusable.

The grapes, at this point, are like raisins, and a minute amount of juice is present in them. The Botrytis even saps more of this juice from the grape, thus concentrating the sugars even more. Add to this, the fact that Botrytis itself infuses into the grape a honey-apricot and lime flavor, and you can see why the price of a wine that is saturated with Botrytis will bring much more money at the marketplace compared to ones without the "noble rot."

Germany makes some outstanding dessert wines. In Germany, the level of sweetness is strictly regulated, and all the grapes marked with a particular designation have exact amounts of sugar as dictated and prescribed by law. German wines marked "auslese" appearing after the name of the town and the vineyard—means the grapes were "out-picked," or picked out of, or, after harvest. This is the same as late harvest. These wines are richly sweet, and go well for sipping and desserts.

Germany doesn't stop here, however, and the further classifications of beerenauslese, trockenbeerenauslese, and eiswein are progressively sweeter, and on the restaurant wine list they will be progressively more expensive. They are normally sold in splits, or half-bottles which contain about 12 ounces of wine. Check with the sommelier on the size of the bottle.

To review the information on the specific sweetness levels of German wine, go back and read the section "How To Read A Wine Label." This will give you all the necessary information about the German designations and what they mean.

In Bordeaux, France, the areas called "Sauternes" and "Barsac" make some of the finest dessert wines in the world. While Germany uses the Riesling grape for the super sweet wines, Sauternes and Barsac use two. These grapes are Sauvignon Blanc and Semillon. They are the two grape varieties also used to make the dry white wines of Bordeaux—but in Sauternes, they take on a whole new glorious dimension!

Both of these grapes are susceptible to Botrytis Cinerea—the fungus called the noble rot—and both are high in sugar content. These aspects suit them well for dessert wines of outstanding character and quality. Again, we will go over some of the processes which are used in making dessert wines. This material has been discussed before, but it bears repeating in that the intensive viticultural techniques used really increase the price of the wine. Especially on the restaurant wine list where the price for a half bottle could be astronomical!

As we have stated before, these grapes that form the wine are picked one at a time, and each basket that is filled is marked with the time of day it is picked. Grapes picked in the afternoon have different qualities than the grapes picked in the morning, and then these baskets of individually picked grapes are blended to achieve the taste the winemaker is after. The grape pickers who pick grapes for dessert wines such as Sauternes are very experienced, since a few bad grapes will make the whole batch taste "off". That is why these wines fetch such astronomical prices at the market.

Some of the names of these Sauternes and Barsacs are: Chateau D'Yquem, Chateau Climens, Doisy Daene, Filhot, Guiraud, Rieussec, and Suduiraut.

California also makes excellent dessert wines. Dessert wines here are made from Riesling, Sauvignon Blanc, Semillon, and also Muscat, and even Chardonnay! California has a great climate to allow the grapes to fully ripen, and also the right climate for the formation of Botrytis Cinerea. One creative winemaker even built a huge refrigerated warehouse so he could freeze his grapes and make a type of eiswein! Californians are very inventive. California dessert wines are usually not as expensive as their European counterparts, so it is much easier to just pick up a bottle and try one—you'll be hooked! Try them with just some hunks of semi-sweet chocolate, and hey—when you wake up from that sugar coma, it'll be a whole new week!

Fortified dessert wines like Port and Sherry are made from a different process than the above dessert wines. These wines are called "fortified" because grape brandy is added somewhere along the line. This increases the amount of alcohol to about 21%—most dessert wines are around 16%. When making Port wine—Port, by the way, comes from the Port of Oporto in Portugal—the winemaker starts off with fermenting of the grapes, then, approximately half way through fermentation he adds high proof grape brandy. This immediately kills the yeast and stops fermentation.

A good amount of residual sugar is still in the wine at this point, and with the addition of the grape brandy, you have a beverage which is high in both sugar and alcohol. When a Port is marked "vintage," this means the grapes from that year were declared "exceptional" by a consortium of the growers. "Vintage" Ports are usually more expensive; only 3 or 4 years out of a decade are usually declared a "vintage." When the Port made is not from a vintage year, the name "Port" will be on the label, and just the year, without the word "vintage." Tawny and Ruby Port refer to the age and color. Tawny means "brown" and refers to the color of the Port—darker and browner—because it has been aged in oak casks.

Oak does for Port what it does for other wines—it makes them richer, and smoother, and softer, and rounder, and more expensive! "Ruby" Port— "ruby" meaning "bright red" in color—is younger port that has not been aged. Ruby Ports are a little leaner, are bright red in color, and are less expensive than tawny Ports. Ports are usually offered by the glass by the restaurants because you can open a bottle and just leave it on the bar and it will stay the same—or get better—over the years. Port is already oxidized, so exposing them to air only improves their flavor—keep the cap on however, or the alcohol will evaporate.

Sherry is produced in southern Spain in the city of Jerez (hair-eth), and "Sherry" is an Anglo-Saxonized pronunciation of this city. Sherry is made from a grape called Palomino. The grapes are fermented as usual, and after fermentation, a mixture of high proof brandy and late harvest grape must containing large amounts of sugar, is added to the wine. If a drier Sherry is sought, less of the grape must high in sugar is used, if a sweeter sherry is wanted, more of the must will be added.

In Port, brandy was added during fermentation when there was still sugar left unfermented in the wine. With Sherry, since the wine is allowed to ferment fully, sugar must be added since it has all been turned to alcohol. After this mixture is added, the wine is put into 158 gallon oak casks, and arranged in a system of rows called a "Solera." This is a system in which the older Sherries are fractionally blended with the younger Sherries, and new Sherries are added each year. As the Sherry gets older, less and less is added until only very small amounts of the oldest wine is blended.

In the meantime, the newly added wines continue to age, and as they grow older, less and less of them are added. The Solera, therefore, allows a great blend of old wines with the new, and the older the age of the Solera, the older the general age of the Sherry will be, thus offering rich, mature, and very tasty wine! Sherry, like Port, is served by the glass, since it is already oxidized. Old Sherries can last for centuries; they are quite profound.

Ordering Champagne from a wine list is just about as easy as any other of the wines, as long as you observe a few basic rules. First of all, Champagne can be ordered for any number of entrees, or for any number of occasions. Champagne can be ordered as an aperitif, that is, as a drink to "open your appetite," or, as part of the meal with entrees like crab, lobster, or any rich fish. Champagne goes exceedingly well with caviar, and just as many other combinations that you can think of. Be creative!

Champagne is made from the Chardonnay grape, or from the Pinot Noir grape if a fruitier taste is desired. The wine is then refermented and the carbon dioxide gas which is formed during fermentation is locked inside the bottle the wine is fermenting in. Instead of escaping through a fermentation lock like in regular winemaking, the carbon dioxide gas gets trapped literally inside the wine itself. This gives the wine its carbonation or "fiz". Champagne is simply a fine white or rose' wine that is "sparkling".

Since Champagne is a region in France that makes this style of wine, only those bottles coming from the Champagne region say "Champagne" on the label. California "Champagne" is simply another way of saying California "sparkling wine"—again, like "Burgundy" and "Chablis" that comes from California, this is just another way of California vintners giving their wine some name recognition.

When ordering, if you want a bright, crisp, and snappy sparkling wine or Champagne, order a blanc de blanc. This means "white wine from a white grape" and denotes that the blend is 100% Chardonnay. Chardonnay is a white grape. If you would like a fruitier and richer tasting sparkling wine or Champagne, then order blanc de noir—"white wine from a black grape". This tells you that the blend is 100% Pinot Noir, which is a black grape. The wine will be a deeper color, however it will not be dark red like the wine made from the grape, since the contact time, or the time the juice stays in contract with the skin to absorb color and flavor, is not very long; it is just enough time to pick up an amber color.

The sparkling wine or Champagne which has neither "blanc de blanc" nor "blanc de noir" is a blend of the two grapes, and the flavor is somewhere between crisp and lively, and rich and fruity, depending on the percent of each grape. Most of California's top sparkling wine makers use only Pinot Noir and Chardonnay—the same used in the Champagne region.

Dryness levels of sparkling wines range from bone dry to sweet. But in a sparkling wine, these designations are quite different. "Natural" is a term given to a sparkling wine or Champagne which is absolutely bone dry—no sugar at all. Brut is next with about 1.5% residual sugar, and "extra dry" is actually the least dry of the dry classification with about 2.5% residual sugar. In the sweet range, "semisweet" contains about 4% residual sugar and sweet anywhere from 5% to 7% residual sugar.

Champagne also comes in different grades of quality. "Methode' Champenoise" is the best way to make Champagne. It will also say "Fermented in *this* bottle" when made from this process. The second best way to make champagne is called "the transfer method" and will say "fermented in *the* bottle." The least best way to make champagne is called the "Charmat Process"—it is vat fermented.

When made the methode' champenoise way, the wine is transferred right to the permanent bottle immediately after fermentation, but with a temporary cap. The winemaker will add a tirage—a combination of yeast, wine and sugar—to start a secondary fermentation. This secondary fermentation produces carbon dioxide gas and is not allowed to escape. The gas intermixes with the wine and the "fiz" is produced.

After this process, the bottles are continually turned so that all the sediment from the secondary fermentation process eventually collects in the neck of the bottle. This is called "riddling." The temporary cap is removed along with the collection of dead yeast and sediment. This is called "disgorging". The winemaker now adds a "dosage." This "dosage" is a mixture of sugar and wine, and the amount that is added will determine the Champagne's final sweetness level. If the winemaker adds nothing, then the Champagne will be naturally dry and classified as "Natural." If he adds 1.5% sugar, the champagne will be labeled "brut," and if he adds 2.5%, the final blend will be labeled "extra dry."

The transfer method entails taking the wine out of the bottle after secondary fermentation has taken place and placed in a vat. The wine is filtered, the dosage is added for the sweetness level, and then the wine is placed in another bottle for the marketplace.

That is why the label will say "fermented in *the* bottle" and not *this* bottle—it has been removed from the original bottle. Fermenting and keeping the wine in the original bottle is much more work intensive, but more of the delicate flavors are kept in the wine if it stays in the same bottle in which it has undergone its secondary fermentation in. The least best way to make a sparkling wine is the Charmat or vat process. Secondary fermentation takes place in a vat rather than a bottle. The wine is filtered and placed in a bottle and is ready for sale.

A Champagne's "bead" is the fineness and persistence of the bubble. A Champagne should be rich and creamy—the bead fine and persisting for a long time in the glass. If the bubbles are very big, and the wine is very gassy, then the Champagne does not have a good bead and is of lesser quality. If you order Champagne, the wine should be brought chilled, and an ice bucket supplied, along with a stand or other apparatus that allows you to keep the wine cold as it is consumed, but not have it on the table where you are eating.

The cork should swell up to where it is impossible to ever get it back into the bottle. If the cork is easily replaced after it is removed, you have about a ninety percent chance that the wine is bad. You can tell because it will have a cardboard taste, and the "fiz" will be all but gone. The wine said to be "flat" or bad. Always check the cork with champagne.

REVIEW AND REITERATION
PART SIX

■ Glass Pours are usually inferior and generic wine. Unless the restaurant is featuring a glass pour from a distinguished winemaker, stay away from these if you are serious about wine.

■ "Chablis" and "Burgundy" when in the "glass pour" section are merely euphemisms for white and red wine, respectively. These generic blends use the French term for name recognition and are not from those regions in France.

■ Good, delicately sweet wines include Chenin Blanc (Vouvray is French Chenin Blanc), Muscat (Asti Spumante is a good example), Rieslings come in a number of varying sweetness levels and are all easy to drink (German wines are all made from Rieslings or its hybrids), and White Zinfandel.

■ Chardonnays (French counterpart is White Burgundy), Sauvignon Blanc (French counterparts are Sancerre and Pouilly Fume), Semillon, and most Italian whites such as Trebbiano, Gavi, and Pinot Grigio are all dry white wines. Chardonnays will have the most depth and breeding—and because they are oaked, will usually be buttery and soft.

■ More expensive wines are usually from grapes whose yield per acre is limited to 2 or 3 tons per acre, instead of the usual 5 or 6 tons per acre.

■ More expensive wines are usually oaked more lavishly, since oak really gives a lot of rich and buttery flavors to wine. Some wine purists will argue that if you spend a lot of money on growing fantastic grapes, then you should taste those grapes—not the barrel.

■ Sommeliers are there to help you enjoy what you like—not what they like. Order what you want, if you need suggestions, and trust the sommelier, then follow his lead—otherwise, be the boss.

■ Cabernets and Merlots (French counterparts are the Red Bordeaux) are dry red wines. Pinot Noirs (French counterpart is Red Burgundy) are softer, but can be really good, or really bad.

■ Beaujolais is a soft and fruity red wine. Although they are dry, they have much less tannin than regular red wine, and therefore will be much less puckery.

■ In Bordeaux, wine is classified by a system of "growths." First growth is the best, second growth is second best, third growth is rated third, etc.

REVIEW AND REITERATION
PART SIX

■ In Burgundy, top wines will be given either Grand Cru classification or Premier Cru classification. Sometimes they will state towns and vineyards like Puligny-Montrachet, or Chasagne Montrachet, etc., these wines are the mark of superlative quality.

■ Generally, in France, the more specific the origin—town, vineyard, etc.—the better the wine.

■ As a guideline, red wines with red meats, and white wines with white meats. This is only a guideline. Drink what you like with what food you like.

■ Pouilly-Fuisse, Meursault, all the Montrachets, most Macons, are all made out of the Chardonnay grape.

■ Italian reds are some of the most intense in the world—especially those made of the Nebbiolo grape. These are Barolo, Barbaresco, and Gattinara. They come from a region called Piedmont.

■ Tuscany makes great Italian wines also. Tuscany uses the grape called Sangiovese and makes Chianti, Brunello di Montalcino and Vino Nobile di Montepulciano.

■ Sweet dessert wines are exotic and you should not exclude these very important wines as part of your dining experiences—they can be as profound as the most expensive and oldest red wines.

■ Germany makes excellent dessert wines. Beerenauslese, trocken-beerenauslese, and eiswein are all superb examples.

■ France's contribution to the dessert wines of the world are called Sauternes.

■ All dessert wines depend on the fungus Botrytis Cinerea, and a host of climactic conditions all present at specific times to make outstanding wine. These conditions may only all be present once or twice in a decade.

■ California makes excellent "Late Harvest" wines from a variety of grapes. California dessert wines tend to be less expensive than the French or German counterparts.

■ Ports or Sherries are fortified wines, because they are fortified with both high proof grape brandy, and in the case of Sherry, sweet grape juice or wine.

REVIEW AND REITERATION
PART SIX

■ Champagne or sparkling wine has undergone a secondary fermentation in which the carbon dioxide gas is not allowed to escape, so it gets caught between the molecules of wine, and give it its "fiz".

■ Tirage is the name of the yeast and sugar and wine mixture that starts secondary fermentation.

■ Methode Champenoise is the most expensive way to make Champagne. Secondary fermentation takes place in the same bottle it is sold in and will say "Fermented in **this** bottle".

■ The transfer method is the second best way to make Champagne. Secondary fermentation takes place inside a bottle, the wine is then transferred to a vat where it is fined and filtered. It is then put in another bottle for sale. Will say "fermented in **the** bottle."

■ Charmat or vat method—the champagne is fermented in a big vat, and then is placed in the bottle. It is the least expensive way to make Champagne.

■ Champagne should be rich and creamy—if it has gigantic bubbles— the wine does not have a lot of grace and breeding.

■ Riddling is a process of slowly turning the bottles (Methode Champenoise Method) so that the sediment from secondary fermentation collects at the neck.

■ Disgorgement is the process of removing the sediment from riddled bottles.

PART SEVEN

Health Aspects of Wine

PRONUNCIATION GUIDE
PART SEVEN

Resveratrol (rez ver´ a trol)
A substance contained in the tannin of the grape that is manufactured as a response to attacks by fungus in the vineyard. This substance also has been found to have a beneficial effect on blood cholesterol.

Anti-oxidants (an tee oks e dents)
Compounds such as those contained in the tannin of grape, and vitamins such as vitamin "C" and "E" and Beta Carotene which scavenge the body of disease-causing free radicals.

Free radicals (free rad e kals)
Produced when the body is exposed to harmful substances and also produced by oxygen-using tissues as waste material. They are disease and cancer causing entities that damage cell DNA and therefore alter the message that assures normal growth.

Quercetin (kwer´ sa tin)
Chemical found in wine, garlic, and onions that is a potent cancer fighter.

PART SEVEN

Health Aspects of Wine

Every year in the United States, 464 out of every 100,000 people die of coronary artery disease. In France, this figure is much lower—about 310 people per 100,000—even though most Frenchmen get little exercise other than walking, and smoking is much more of a problem there than it is here. The French also eat more saturated fat in the form of cheeses and goose fat, and their intake of olive oil is much higher than ours. What, then, accounts for the lower death rate, with risk factors that we consider to be quite indicitive of what we might call the "heart attack profile"?

Many people think it has to do with the amount of wine they drink. Red Wine. Until recently, the active ingredient in wine was thought to be the alcohol, but studies have shown that although alcohol does have a positive effect on platelet aggregation and the lowering of LDL (bad) cholesterol, the level in your blood has to be about that approaching legal drunkenness—0.1%. Since most people don't approach this level on a daily basis, researchers began looking for another factor that might cause Frenchmen to have better chances of avoiding heart disease. At about this same time, it was discovered that the same ingredient used in lowering cholesterol from an ancient Chinese cure was the same ingredient that had just been isolated by botanists as having a beneficial effect on blood level cholesterol.

The compound was tannin—the part of the grape just under the skin and before the pulp—and the specific elements of this compound were beginning to be isolated. Scientists believe there are over 100 active substances in the tannin of grape skin, and about 20 of these have been identified. One of the most potent is called resveratrol. Resveratrol is formed by the grape to fight off fungus infestation in the vineyard. This substance then stays in the grape tannin and is released and concentrated during fermentation. You would have to drink about 20 ounces of grape juice to get the same effect as about 4 ounces of wine.

Also, grape juice is usually filtered to clarify it and make it more appealing. Most red wines are only lightly filtered because most of the great taste of red wine is contained in the particles that are filtered out. Also, fermentation greatly changes the chemical compound of the juice so that it is much more biologically active. Also contained in the tannin of the grape are anti-oxidants. These compounds scavenge the body for free radicals. Free radicals are cancer causing agents that slam into cells over and over and cause, by constant irritation, disease and the aging process as we know it. The fewer the free radicals in our bodies, the healthier we will be. Beta carotene, the deep coloring in carrots, sweet potatoes, kale, and most vegetables, contains anti-oxidants. Vitamin "E" is an anti-oxidant, and so is vitamin "C."

Wine is reported to have higher levels of biologically active antioxidants than any of these vitamins. This is one of the ways it keeps cholesterol from oxidizing and changing to bad cholesterol. These compounds are also responsible for preventing irritants—free radicals and the like—from scaring arterial walls. Once the walls on the inside of arteries are abraded, cholesterol tries to pack against these abrasions and forms plaque build-ups. Over a period of time, this plaque gets hard and callused, and even starts to contain blood vessels because the body is trying to support new tissue which it thinks is healing on abrasion.

These build-ups become bigger and bigger over time and close off the blood supply that the heart needs. A heart attack results. Red wine consumed daily prevents both the scaring and the tendency for cholesterol to build up on the artery walls. These anti-oxidants also play a role in preventing other diseases. Cancer is probably the most feared word in the English—or any other—language. But, high doses of anti-oxidants in for form of beta carotene and the chemicals contained in wine have dramatically reduced both initial formation, and the process that allows it to spread once it has struck.

One of the elements in wine, quercetin, is a powerful cancer fighter. It is the same element that is the active ingredient in garlic and onions. As studies continue to emerge, and information is digested and assililated, certain thoughts about wine become proven facts.

In the Danish Study, Morten Gronbaek and his five compatriots separated wine drinkers from beer and liquor drinkers. They discovered that while the beneficial effects of beer and liquor begin to once again become negative after two beers or two ounces of liquor, wine drinkers who had up to five glasses—or five "drinks", which is about 25 ounces of wine—had no similar negative effects. In fact, in Denmark, where heart disease was at one time one of the of the highest levels per capita in the world, they discovered a 30% decline in the disease over a fifteen year period. They also discovered, that in the same period of time, wine consumption increased 30%. This direct correlation was investigated and it was discovered that people who drank the most wine, had the fewest heart attacks, and had the least amount of heart disease. People who drank beer had a smaller amount of heart disease, and people who drank large amounts of liquor, actually had greater mortality rates from all causes.

But with wine, the protective effects seem to be dose related, and the study included 3 to 5 glasses of wine per day—with risk factors going down with every glass. This information was reported in the British Medical Journal in May, 1995. Some of the facts emerging from other studies show that people who drank wine every day had a 40% reduced risk of adult onset diabetes, 50% reduced risk of heart attack, 25% reduced risk of the most common type of stroke, dramatically reduced risk of gallstones, and a significant reduction of upper respiratory infections (colds). Others are concerned that making this information known will cause a serious increase in alcohol consumption and therefore increases in cirrhosis of the liver.

The fact is, that in parts of the world where more wine is consumed, cirrhosis rates are lower than that of the United States. For example, in southern France, little beer or liquor is consumed, but much wine. Cirrhosis rates are about 7 per 100,000. Compare this with the United States at 15 cirrhosis deaths per 100,000, or, in Northern France where much more beer and liquor is consumed, and cirrhosis rates are about 30 per 100,000. (Compare this rate with that of the toll heart disease takes at 464 per 100,000 in the United States, and, with a little arithmetic, you can see that wine consumption will not only reduce heart attacks, but probably maintain cirrhosis rates at the present level.) These statistics are from the World Health Organization.

Another beneficial effect of alcohol, and especially wine, was found to be among senior citizens and the way they interacted with each other. Senior citizens who had one to three glasses of wine per day were much more social, and had more friends and a larger support group than those who drank nothing at all. This information was also found to be true in all ages—again, especially with wine—that people who gathered together with food, where wine was part of the meal, were much likelier to be part of each others daily routine. People talked to each other more often, were more likely to share information and events—both good and bad—and were also much more likely to live longer. Certain aspects of wine are tending to emerge. One is, the fact that wine, when consumed with food, gets into the blood stream much more slowly, and therefore blood alcohol levels—which may be one of the main indicators of toxicity and therefore risk factors—was at a much lower level over a period of time.

Remember, wine is also a food, and is absorbed in the intestines, and not in the stomach. This delay gives a much more gradual increase in blood alcohol levels. Also, wine is basically 100% fruit and therefore contains all the benefits that we normally attribute to those who eat a more plant based—rather than animal based—diet. The stigma attached to wine drinking is beginning to recede, but there are still people out there who would wince at giving their seven year old wine mixed with water. Even though it is a proven fact that wine and water will probably reduce that child's risk of heart disease by as much as 70%.

But, old thoughts die hard, and for some people to allow their children to drink in the home would be out of the question. Family problems with alcoholism and abuse are always at the back of our minds, but the fact is, that when wine is served in the home, and at mealtime with the parents

CONSUMER TIP

Red wine with meals is a proven health benefit. If you cannot drink red wine because it is too dry or bitter, try mixing it with a little sweet wine like a muscat.

Fruits and vegetables should be the staples in the diet with either meat as a small side-dish, for flavoring, or not at all. Most Americans get too much protein from meat, and this is not only difficult to digest and metabolize, but also hard on internal organs like the kidneys which have to deal with all the waste from the protein assimilation.

Family meal time should be a time of sharing. Wine is part of the process of sharing, caring. Interpersonal relationships are strengthened and bolstered by mutual nurturing and compassion. No other time is more appropriate for wine than that of meal time. Not to plan the days activities with this thought in mind is like building a house with no furnace or hot water.

Learn as much about wine as you can, and go to wine-friendly establishments and restaurants. In this way, you'll feel easier about having wine in the home. Nothing is scarier than ignorance about something.

in a family centered activity like meals, abuse is much more unlikely. Children taught to enjoy wine with their family are much more centered and grow up understanding the responsibility they have to themselves and other members of both the family and community. Problems arise when wine is looked upon by teenagers—or anyone—as something that makes you get "high" and is therefore forbidden in the home.

When this happens, binge drinking with others who are only there to get drunk result. Most parents look at this as a supporting evidence for forbidding alcohol in the home. But where is a person to learn how to imbibe responsibly? With his teenage friends? With a group out to get a "buz"? With people who have no idea—because no one has ever taught them how to responsibly imbibe—of the detrimental effects of alcohol and no idea of how much is too much? No wander we read of young people dying of alcohol poisoning. We teach our children everything. Why not teach them how to stay healthy and stay alive? Maybe it is too simple. We would rather die of heart attacks, cancer, diabetes. We would rather die of diseases that are "American" and just shrug our shoulders when asked why is brother 200 pounds overweight. Doing things that are intelligent and take some thought are threatening to a lot of people. They would rather have someone tell them that this product or thing is all good or all bad.

But when something comes along that takes a bit of thought, and this same product has the potential to be as lethal as it is good, then most people fold up like big circus tents and go home. The reason? They have to think and decide, and if they are wrong, they are responsible—and who in this day and age wants to be responsible? So wine, like a lot of other things takes some thought, some deliberation, some study, and some effort to understand. For some people, this is a monumental undertaking. They would rather just not have to deal with it.

No problem. There will be more wine for the rest of us, and these people will muddle through their mediocre lives cringing in the corner every time a decision that could improve their lives confronts them. They will suffer for themselves, and their children will suffer from not being taught how to effectively arrive at a decision. I wouldn't be so insistent on these points if there wasn't a secondary aspect to them. This aspect is in dealing with the decision making process, and what it teaches everyone in the home. Abdicating responsibility because of one's inability to "take the bull by the horns" reinforces this attitude, and children leave the home in the morning not knowing how to solve problems. They either wait till they go away—which they don't—or they totally decide not to deal with problems—like their parents.

Children will form the opinions that their parents have, and when something is shunned because the parents are afraid to deal with it, children learn that this product, wine in this case, is either bad, and therefore will at some point be used irresponsibly and in excess outside the home, or, used with no thought at all as to its efficacy or danger. Family centered activities in which all feel comfortable sharing their fears and problems—including the parents—are ideal ways to come up with not only solutions, but a thought process for dealing with problems that results in less problems.

Drinking wine in the home could be dangerous. Parents can't hand their kids a bottle of wine and say "go to it." This, like all other activities takes time, and an attitude of thoughtfulness based on a good feeling by both teacher and student. This feeling is fostered in the home when both parent and child arrive at a solution together. The child feels as if he is brought the information necessary to make a decision by someone who has a great interest in his well-being. This feeling is reinforced and returned to family members and friends. The results are that both the child and the parent shared in a thoughtful and creative decision making event, and both benefited.

These types of attitudes foster a feeling that one is worth the time and the effort and children begin to grow balanced and centered. These attitudes are "caught"—not taught—in the home, and reinforced at school. They are reinforced by good teachers who understand the importance of showing students how to solve problems, and not by teaching them to hide from them.

Wine in the home is no problem for people who want to share in its benefits with other family members. And there is earnest interest in each others well-being, formation, growth, and happiness. Wine in the home IS a problem when it is irresponsibly given, and with no instruction or discipline or direction by the parents. Hey, be the boss—but be loving and be thoughtful, and be disciplined. And, teach your children; don't leave it up to someone else.

REVIEW AND REITERATION
PART SEVEN

- Heart attacks kill 464 out of every 100,000 people each year. Wine will decrease this risk by about 50% when consumed regularly and with meals.

- Wine also decreases mortality rates from other diseases as well. Cancer, colds, gallstones, diabetes are all dramatically reduced with normal and regular consumption.

- Wine contains some of the most powerful anti-oxidants known to man.

- Wine drinkers seem to be able to increase their health benefits with increased consumption—up to three to five glasses or 15 to 25 ounces of wine. Beer and whiskey drinkers seem to negate the benefits of drinking after only two drinks—with mortality risks increasing after more than two.

- Neo-prohibitionists worried of the abuse of alcohol have played down the benefits of wine lumping it in with "drugs" or whiskey and beer. This is a big disservice to the American population who look to people in authority for guidance.

- Wine gets into the blood stream much more slowly than whiskey and beer, and therefore, blood level alcohol—a determining factor of toxicity—never reaches dangerous levels, when consumed in moderate amounts with food.

- As in all things, education is the key to success. Learning more about wine will help you decide how to teach your family the proper way to consume it. Example is the best teacher.

- Family centered activities with strong role models teach children discipline. In this atmosphere, abuse is much less likely.

PART EIGHT

Wine Accoutrements: Glassware, Cork Removers, etc.

PRONUNCIATION GUIDE
PART EIGHT

Auger (ah ger)
Drill-like mechanism that pierces the cork on the wine opener.

Decanting (dee kant ing)
Process of pouring wine from the bottle into another container to remove the sediment and allow it to breathe.

Sediment (sed a ment)
Collection of dead yeast, and larger particles of tannin, that collect in the bottom or side of a bottle of wine.

PART EIGHT

Wine Accoutrements

· ·

Opening, Pouring, Decanting And Tasting—
Wine Paraphernalia And Accoutrements

The first matter at hand is to get the wine out of the bottle. To do this, the cork must be removed. Simple. Sometimes. Cork removing devices range from relatively easy and inexpensive to rather intriguing and expensive. The best, though admittedly not the least expensive are the Screwpulls. These have fine, sharp augers that drill through the cork without destroying it the way some augers do.

Look at the auger (the drill-like screw bit that pierces the cork) and see if the one that you have is sharp and fine, or, thick with a dull point. If it is the thick with a dull point, it will invariably ruin the cork, and make extracting it a messy job. The Screwpull is about fifteen to twenty dollars— depending on where you shop. The Screwpull has a sturdy plastic body that fits over the neck of the bottle.

Next, the auger is inserted into the body which guides it into the cork. As you twist or turn the top of the auger, it anchors itself against the bottle and as you twist, the leverage created pulls the cork out of the bottle with a screw action. It is simple and ingenious, and it works well.

Some people like the two-bladed cork extractor called the "ah-so". I guess this is suppose to be short for "ah so easy" in regards to removing the cork. Every time I use one I end up saying not "ah so", but "ah" and the next word rhymes with "it"—because I always push the cork into the bottle and wine squeezes up past the cork and squirts in my face and on my hair and shirt.

But, for those of you who are more intelligent, or dexterous or what- ever it takes, they are about four or five dollars. One blade is longer than the other, and you start by inserting the longer blade in between the cork and the bottle neck. When it is in about an eighth of an inch, insert the other blade on the other side of the cork. Rock the handle back and forth until the blades are past the cork, and then with a twisting motion of the wrist, pull up. Don't push the blades straight down, this will push the cork into the bottle 100% of the time, but doing it the right way—rocking it back and forth and then pulling up with a twisting motion—will only push the cork into the bottle 60% of the time. The "ah-so" is also called the "butler's friend", supposedly because these handy gizmos allowed a butler to steal wine out of a bottle and replace the cork without damaging the cork, and therefore escaping the wrath of his master who could not possibly know the butler stole any of his wine, even though the bottle is half empty.

Another device is the wing tip cork screw. With these, you have an auger and a set of wings that gradually rise to a position of erection (for lack of a better term) and then when the auger is fully inserted and the wings are "all the way up" you grab them and pull down on them, this in turn ejects the cork. The augers on these "wing types" are sometimes too fat and ruin the cork. The waiter's blade is next. this is the Swiss army knife of openers, and comes with a knife for cutting the foil, and an auger that drills into the cork. The other metal extension—which also serves as a bottle cap remover is then placed on the lip of the bottle, and with an upward lift, creates leverage which yanks the cork from the bottle.

These openers are pretty good—unless you get a defective bottle which cracks off at the neck when you apply the force that creates the leverage that extracts the cork. These are pretty nifty and for some reason feel good in your hand. It must remind us of our caveman days when we felt secure with a knife in our hands. This knife, however, is so small that it would really just make someone extremely mad if you tried to stab anybody with it—probably mad enough that he might do you great bodily harm and injure parts of your body that you wouldn't want emergency room people to see unless you were dying.

Another type of cork removing device works on compressed air. A long needle is inserted down through the cork into the bottle. You then push the button on top to release carbon dioxide from a cartridge contained in the body of the mechanism, which creates pressure within the bottle and pushes the cork up.

Or, you pump air into the bottle from a pump located on the top which enters the bottle via the hollow needle—just like the CO^2 type—and again, the cork is forced out of the bottle. Still other types of corkscrews consist of stands which hold a bottle of wine, and with a lever that is pulled down, pierces the cork, and then extracts it. These are all brass, or bronze, and run anywhere from 70 to 150 dollars. These also attach to countertops. I have one. I love it. The only thing that is inconvenient is taking off the capsule—they should have a foil cutter on the table model somewhere.

Foil cutters, by the way, consist of four little sharp wheels, which when placed on the top lip of the neck of the bottle, over the foil, will cut the foil off and reveal the cork. The foil or capsule protects the cork from dirt and the like, and must be removed before the cork is taken out, although I have to confess that I've drilled right into the cork on occasion without removing the foil, and then removed the foil after the cork made a hole on the top. Sometimes I'm rascally.

Once the cork is removed from the bottle, you may want to decant. Decanting is the process of taking the wine out of the bottle slowly, trying to leave the sediment at the bottom or on the side of the bottle, and transferring the wine into another container for airing.

There is a device into which you put the bottle for this purpose and then light a candle which is set underneath the neck of the bottle. The candle then allows you to see the wine clearly as it is slowly poured via a catapult-like mechanism which slowly raises the back of the bottle by turning the screw. As the wine is slowly poured, any particles or sediment can easily be seen as you peer through the illuminated neck. You can stop turning the screw which will immediately stop the pouring and therefore keep the sediment in the bottle.

Why do you want to remove the sediment? Well, some people do not like chunks of stuff floating around in their wine. I kind of like it, so I

CONSUMER TIP

Investing in good stem ware is one of the most rewarding aspects of wine drinking. You cannot imagine how a good glass really allows you to taste all the flavors of a wine. Riedel and other manufacturers usually make a number of different glasses for red, white and sparkling wines. They also make glasses at different price points. This allows you to buy glasses that fit into your budget.

Long stems and thinner glass seem to make the wine more elegant, and while thicker glass is certainly more durable and dishwasher friendly, too thick a glass feels clumsy in your hand and, for some reason, doesn't allow the wine to show its best. On the other hand, very expensive glasses are about as fragile as potato chips, and crack or just plain break with even the slightest nudge. These are pretty, but not really usable on the day-to-day basis. Somewhere in-between is the perfect glass — a nice large bowl, sturdy but not overly heavy or clumsy in your hand, and, dishwasher friendly. Buy these!

never decant unless I get an old Port with about three inches of junk in the bottom of the bottle, and then I just don't pour any more when I see that most of my glass looks like sediment. Some people are upset by any amount of stuff in their wine. In this case, bring a coffee filter or a hankey and pour the wine through this—this ·will remove **all** the sediment. The decanter should be an open-mouthed pitcher-like pourer which will open the volume of wine to the air. In this way, some of the sulfur-like aromas will "blow off" and the wine will "breathe"—oxygen will mix with the wine and enhance its flavor.

If you let old wines in the decanter too long, you may end up with a very thin washed out wine-like substance that once used to be wine. Remember, old wines may be at their peak, and airing them—which is akin to aging them—may push them into oblivion. (Does that rhyme?) Younger wines may be left in the decanter longer and will usually profit from the airing. Italian wines like Barolos and Barbarescos need at least three or four hours in the decanter, and the remnants left in the corner by some guest that you found four days later will probably be just right to drink. After proper decanting and airing/breathing, the wine is now ready to be poured into a glass. The choice of glasses is huge.

Finding The Right Glass

For red wines, a nice big bowl and a slightly narrower lip will both exposes the wine to air and then focus its sweet perfume directly into your nose. A narrower rim also allows you to swirl without getting wine on the next three people standing by you. I like glasses that hold about 25 ounces, and usually pour about two ounces at a time. This gives me enough room in the glass to get a good swirl going and really mixes air with the wine. The brand names of glasses that you can buy all boast of making wine taste better, and this is true. You need proper stemware and glassware to get all the flavor and nuances that good wines contain. Riedel Crystal is one company that makes wine glasses for red wines, white wines, Champagnes, and they come in different price ranges to fit all budgets.

Before I pour wine in any glass, I always smell it. Just stick your honker deep down in the glass and take a big whif. Are there any strange odors in the glass? A hunk of old tomato left from the sink or dishwasher? Any detergents smells, or odors from the cupboard? All these, obviously, will detract from the wine. Check the glass before you pour your wine. For

Champagne, use a smaller glass that holds about 6 or 7 ounces and is tall and thin. These glasses expose the least amount of wine to the air, and therefore will not permit the escape of the carbon dioxide bubbles—the wine will not go "flat" as fast.

White wines can be drunk out of the same wine glasses that red wines are drunk. White wine glasses, however, tend to be a little smaller, but, I think a big rich Chardonnay tastes better from the red wine glass. What about paper cups, plastic cups, jars, etc. As long as there are no strange odors in the glass, and as long as the glass is clear. Colored glasses are not for wine, they are for grape juice. Make sure your glasses are clear.

Paper cups are OK in a pinch if there's nothing else around and you disdain drinking from the bottle. And personally, I think plastic makes wine taste funny, but again, if it's not appropriate for stemware because you're outside or whatever and glasses are not available, other containers are OK—as long as they don't ruin the taste of the wine. For fine wine, however, drinking from anything other than good stemware is a sin, and will certainly not allow you to taste the wines as they should be tasted.

Serving Temperature

Red wines served too cold will taste inhibited and will not have much flavor. This is because red wines are much more volatile at room temperature which allows some of the nuances, flavors and aromas to etherize and fill your nose with their scents. Also, in your mouth, these scents will float up the back of your throat into your sinuses and allow you to register a lot of the flavors of the wine via your olfactory sense. Tasting wine "through your nose" and combining this with the information on your taste buds, gives you a more integrated view of the wine.

Red wine should be about 55 degrees, but the more tannin, the more cooler temperatures—under 55 degrees—will inhibit it. Red wines with little tannin, like Beaujolais, can be served a little cooler without making them unpleasant, or hurting their flavor. Red wines served too warm will be unpleasant and taste dull.

White wines are not as volatile as red wines, therefore chilling them will not hurt the way we experience their flavor. 45 to 50 degrees allows you to both taste the wine, and have the coolness refresh your mouth. I've noticed that although tasting Chardonnay at room temperatures reveals a lot of their flavors, drinking them colder offers your mouth a poignant mix of warm toasty flavors, contrasting nicely with the coolness of the wine itself.

Champagne and sparkling wines should be served cold. They are refreshing, and the lower temperatures keeps the carbon dioxide (bubbles) in the wine longer. Tableside, Champagne should always be in a bucket containing water and ice. This will keep it cold. All ice will not keep it as cold as ice and water. Water envelopes the bottle and pulls the heat from it better than ice alone.

REVIEW AND REITERATION
PART EIGHT

- Screwpulls are the cork removers with very sharp and thin augers that extract the cork smoothly and easily. They are easy to use.

- Waiter's blades are a bit harder to use, but are compact and durable.

- Wing-type cork removers sometimes have big, dull augers which invariably ruin the cork.

- The "ah so" or "butler's friend" is good if the cork is not real tight, or, you have great experience using it.

- Table top lever action openers work well. They are the Cadillac of openers, and their price ranges from 70 to over 100 dollars.

- Openers that inject air into the bottle via a hollow needle are nifty, but maintaining them with CO_2 cartridges and keeping the needle from leaking the air that is supposed to go into the bottle, might be a problem.

- Foil cutters are small plastic devices with four cutting wheels that when placed over the neck of the bottle and twisted, will cut the foil and allow it to be removed, exposing the cork.

- Decanting is the act of pouring the wine slowly from the bottle into another container to both remove the sediment, and allow the wine to breathe, before consumption.

- Decanting allows oxygen to be mixed with the wine, greatly speeding up the aging process. This allows a wine to be tasted at its best. Old wines should not be decanted too long—they may be eviscerated.

- Proper glassware is very important to tasting wine.

- Bigger glasses that hold at least 20 ounces are good for red wine. Slightly smaller ones for white wine. Make sure the rim is smaller than the bowl—this allows you to swirl without letting the wine escape, and also focuses the aromas of the wine into your nose.

- Use tall thin glasses for Champagne. This allows a smaller volume of wine to be exposed to the air, allowing the wine to keep its bubbles for a longer period.

- Always smell the glass before you pour the wine into it. Make sure it smells like nothing.

- Paper cups, plastic cups, jars and other types of containers are OK if there are no glasses available, but they usually give wine a funny taste, or at best, don't allow you to taste all the nuances in the wine.

- Red wine should be served at about 55 degrees. White wines at about 45 to 50 degrees, and Champagnes and sparkling wines at 35 degrees.

PART NINE

Buying Strategies and How to Store Wine

PRONUNCIATION GUIDE
PART NINE

Hygrometer (hy grom´ a ter)
Instrument used for measuring water
vapor in the air.

PART NINE

Buying Strategies, Storing Wine

I remember a cartoon in a magazine. A man was standing in the midst of his gigantic wine cellar with his arm around his son, saying, "Hopefully, when I'm gone, none of this will be here, to be yours." Although we enjoy leaving things to our progeny, buying more wine than you can possibly use in two lifetimes just isn't a practical thing to do. Unless, of course, you don't mind spending enormous amounts of money on something you will never have the pleasure of experiencing. Some people just enjoy buying wine. They see rare bottles, and bottles they know will be worth triple the purchase amount in a couple of years, so the temptation to buy these is great. Others look upon wine collecting as a hobby.

Like collecting rare stamps, buying rare wine to hold as "treasures" certainly is satisfying. Still others drink a lot of wine, and buying a lot of it is very practical. We go through a lot of wine at home when guests drop over. Wine is never wasted at our house. But a buying strategy is in order if you don't know what to buy, or if you've just started drinking and collecting and you need a bit of advice. So, here it is.

Ask yourself some questions first. What kind of wine do I like? How much money do I have to spend? These are the two most important questions. Others follow from it. Where will my wine be kept? Is the place I've set aside adequately cooled and humidified? These are the questions you have to realistically answer, otherwise your wine buying will end up sporadic, or unpleasant because you will either have too much wine of one kind, or spend too little on the kind that you like, with no good place to put any of it.

Do you like dry reds? If the answer is yes, you'll want to establish a price range for some short term drinkers, and a few wines to age (over ten years). The seven to twelve dollar range is a good range for everyday wines. You can find a lot of quality in this range, and from the thirteen and fifteen dollar range upwards, depending on your pocketbook, you will be able to find some nice agers. If you like dry white wines, the choice in the price ranges will be about the same, but remember, since white wine has little or no tannin, only the acid and alcohol hold it together, and for long aging, some of the California Chardonnays are so plush and smooth from the deliberate use of riper grapes to keep the acid levels low, that the wines will not age past 12 or 18 months.

The style of Chardonnay now popular is that big, oaky, and very soft up front style. Big and lush, with low acid levels. These are great for short term drinking, but they fall apart in the long haul. Some of the more expensive Montrachets and Grand Crus are the best choice for longer aging, and certainly the sweet white wines of Sauternes and Barsac will age for decades—remember, sugar is a natural preservative. As to how long some of the Grand Crus and Premier Crus will age, depends on the vintage year. Check Parker's Guide for the best vintages for Aging.

Robert Parker is one of the best wine writers in the world. He has a publication called *The Wine Advocate* that is published once every two months. He often repeats printing the vintage chart in the back with updates and revisions on when to drink wine from certain areas. You can subscribe to this publication by writing his office at P.O. Box 311, Monkton, MD 21111.

Champagnes and sparkling wines can age very graciously, becoming extremely rich and tasty with age. Be forewarned, however, that some of the carbon dioxide will pass right through the glass over about ten years, causing your wines to be less carbonated. You will have a great tasting Chardonnay or Pinot Noir though! Buying strategies should also include how much you and your family consume per month; in this way, you can take advantage of the 10% case discounts most retailers give and this will help defray some of the cost.

How much of one wine should you buy? Try not to buy anymore than three or four bottles of one kind at a time. Especially when just starting out, since little or no inventory will doom you to drinking the same wine every night till your store is built up. At first, buy three different brands of the type of wine you enjoy. If you have not tasted the wine, buy one bottle and see if you like the style. Then, when you come back to the store, you can buy three or four more bottles of it. Get used to stopping into your local wine shop. It will be as important as any stop you make if you like wine. Why? Besides getting to know the people there, and exchanging wine stories and shopping for bargains they may wish to extend to better customers, you will see some allocated items that may be put on the shelves in the morning, and be gone that night. Some wineries make precious little wine, and these few bottles are snapped up very quickly by wine buyers savoy enough to keep track of release dates and who may also know the store's owners or buyers.

You will also get used to talking about wine, and the latest and newest wineries, and even meet people who you can invite to your wine tastes, or be invited to theirs. Some good retailers have tasting licenses, and you can actually taste the wine in the store before you buy it. Tasting licenses are a lot of fun, and when the right group gets together in the store, and the owner starts opening different bottles, it can be a very interesting, good time. Be careful driving home, however. Once you get a pretty good inventory, and can drink a different wine every night, you might want to purchase a case of something to put away.

What should be the criteria of buying a case? Number one, do you like the wine? Number two, will the wine appreciate with age, allowing you to sell it if you have outgrown the taste, or no longer want it? Can you afford it? Did you research the wine, and get a little information about it and its history so you know that it will be good to drink when you want to drink it? These questions need to be answered first. If the answer to them satisfies you, make the purchase. If you seem doubtful, at least wait a while, and see if you really still have the urge next week, another good wine may come along by then!

Storing Wine

Wine storage can be as simple or as complex as your buying habits. Like fresh produce, people sometimes enjoy going to the market or the wine store that day to pick the bottle of wine for that night. Or, like a garden, you may enjoy your own stash of vegetables, and wine homegrown from your cellar. Either way, you will probably need to keep wine somewhere, even if it's just short term; for you long termers, the choices will get a little more extravagant.

For short term and long term storage, laying a bottle on the side will assure that the cork stays moist and expanded; assuring a good seal so air will not enter and oxidize the wine. Keep the wine away from heat. Heat will destroy the subtle nuances of flavor in the wine, and ultimately push up the cork and destroy the seal, causing air to enter the bottle. Small add-on racks are popular and keep the wine in a neat orderly fashion. Cubes are nice too, as are wooden shelves or racks. Keep the wine cool, but keeping it in the refrigerator is not the greatest of storage places for anything but short term.

Why? Because refrigerators are usually too cold, and this will make the wine taste blocky and monolithic. Also, refrigerators go into a defrost cycle and the temperature may warm for a while. Irregular temperatures, plus the jarring of opening and shutting the door hundreds of times a day will unsettle the wine. Plus, the humidity is not at the proper level. All of these factors play an important role for wine.

A little too much trouble you think? Remember, wine is not like Hawaiian punch; it is a living, breathing entity, and needs to be properly kept if it is to present you with its flavors in their best possible light. Also, keep the wine out of the sunlight; ultraviolet rays destroy wine. Heaters and other heat sources are bad spots for wine, as is a cupboard space above the stove. A cool North wall is good, or someplace that has cool, even temperatures.

For long term aging, the use of a cellar which has a constant temperature of no more than 55 degrees, and humidity levels at about 70 to 75 degrees is best. Warmer, and the wine will age too quickly and perhaps unevenly. Colder, and they will be in a state of suspended animation, neither maturing nor evolving, but as low as 49 degrees would still be admissible. What about humidity. Humidity needs to be about 70 to 75%. This provides the proper water vapor in the air so that wine will not pass too quickly from the glass into the atmosphere.

Remember, glass is still a permeable substance, and very dry air will cause the wine inside the bottle to pass right through the glass into the atmosphere—the dry and thirsting for moisture atmosphere. This humidity level is also said to be good for the cork, but wine wicked to all parts of the cork from the bottle being laid on its side will keep it moist enough. If the humidity is much past 90%, mold will form on the bottles and corks.

If your cellar does not meet these requirements, and you have a lot of money invested in your wine, you may want to build a wine cellar and then insulate it so that you can cool and humidify properly the interior space. Split systems are ones in which you have a separate compressor in another part of the basement, or outside and a set of pipes carrying the refrigeration to the condensing unit—much like central air. The compressor sits outside, and the refrigeration is pumped in via a copper insulated line that is connected to the condensing unit that sits on top of your furnace. When the blower turns on, it spreads the cool air into your house. A fan and a cooling unit will be located in the wine room itself.

The other type of system is the self-contained system. These units have the compressor and the condensing coils and fan all in the same base—much like a window or room air-conditioner. The difference? In the split system, you can locate the noisy and sometimes heat producing compressor outside; with the self-contained system, you have the whole shbang in the basement, and if you don't mind the sound of the compressor cycling on and off, or the heat it produces you can probably tolerate it.

Humidity can be added to the air via a humidifier. Make sure that you get a hygrometer—an instrument that measures water vapor in the air, and make sure the humidity level is set appropriately. Such wine paraphernalia can be purchased from the same company as the units were

CONSUMER TIP

"The Wine Advocate" by Robert Parker, and "The Wine Spectator", a magazine, are two publications that will help you find wines that are not only ageworthy, but that have the desired attributes you are looking for in wine. Price, for example is as important as the amount of wine produced—this directly affects how easily the wine can be obtained.

There was a list of Spanish wines under ten dollars that "The Wine Spectator" had said were outstanding, but by the time I called to find any, all fifteen of the retailers—and most were in big cities—were out of the wine. Most just laughed when I asked for some of the ones that had received ratings in the nineties and said those were gone before they hit the shelf.

So these publications not only inform you, they also drive the market; they are helpful, nevertheless, because they let you know what is going on in the world of wine. Also, they get you used to the way people talk and describe wine, and this is very helpful. When you drink enough wine, and are used to hearing about a wine that tastes "leathery" and "tobacco-ey," you will eventually experience these concepts of flavor in the wine. These publications, however, can not tell you what to like.

In fact, if you rely too much on these magazines, you are apt to become just another person who thinks ratings are the be-all and the end-all of wine buying, and miss a lot of the very good wine out there just because it wasn't rated.

As in all things, use your own head. Be the chairman of the board, and all the information and knowledge that comes to you is like all the department heads reporting to you. Assimilate all the information, take into consideration your personality and buying habits, your likes and dislikes, and then make a decision—your decision. Let your world be a product of you; not vice versa.

purchased. International Wine Accessories sells such equipment; they are located in Dallas, Texas. To write for their catalogue, use this address: International Wine Accessories, 11020 Audelia Road, Suite B-113, Dallas, Texas 75243.

You can let your imagination run wild if you want to build your own room, then insulate it and add the cooling system instead of buying the whole room already assembled with all the accoutrements. Designing your own room will allow you to custom make your wine room into a labrynth of nooks, crannies, corners, and different levels, all very conducive to an old catacombed wine cellar—even brings back memories of *The Cask of Amontillado,* doesn't it? In addition, you can use a myriad of wine paraphernalia to decorate the room. We know a gentleman who had a 500 gallon oak fermenting barrel shipped from California to his home here in Ohio, and then cut it in half and used these as the entrance to his cellar. He also used nine and fifteen liter bottles to line the entrance way—it was magnificent!

You can let your imagination run wild, and the sky is the limit—as long as it is properly cooled and humidified. Organizing your bottles will be a bit trickier—it is for me, since I don't like to organize my wine, I kind of like to trudge through the different bottles before stumbling onto the right one. But for those of you who want to organize, put the ones you want to age for short term, and the red wines, in one place. Those long agers should also be marked with bottle tags and have the brand and vintage year, also the time by when it should be consumed should also be on the tag. It's also a good idea to put the price of the bottle on the tag, so a guest or neighbor won't grab a 200 dollar bottle of Burgundy for a hot dog bar-b-que.

Wines look nice stored by the case in their original wood containers if possible. Wine rooms with different formats such as a corner for cases, shelves for individual bottles, different sized compartments for both smaller and bigger than 750 ml. bottles, and also room for displays of some of your most prestigious wines are all very popular.

Lighting is also important. Uplighting from the ground, or behind the bottles would be elegant and stunning—don't have any light source directly on a bottle or too close to a bottle—it may over heat the wine. Indirect or different kinds of colors of bulbs all create atmosphere that you are not only proud of, but put you in an attitude and atmosphere conducive of wine—remember, wine is an experience.

Ever wonder why wine tastes better in a dark and elegant restaurant? Yes, it is the big glasses, and the carpet, and the lack of bright lights, and the smell of food, and the fact that you're relaxing—it all adds to your enjoyment. Make something like this for you and your family and guests in your own home. It will probably be a sanctuary for you. A place to go to get away from all the distractions of the day. A place to relax and play and think.

REVIEW AND REITERATION
PART NINE

■ Wine collecting and buying strategies should be determined by your budget and consumption habits.

■ Buying vast amounts of expensive wine requires proper storage facilities either on or off premise.

■ Red wines and sweet dessert wines are best wines to age. Some white wines will not age well; others are good for short and mid-term aging.

■ "The Wine Advocate" by Robert Parker is one of the best subscriptions you can have in your home. He includes vintage dates, and lots of other materials for wine people.

■ Getting to know your local retailer is a good way to learn about wines and find some good buys. It is also a good way to meet other people interested in wine, and learn about wine functions in the community.

■ Wine cellars are a good way to organize your purchases, and assure you that none of your wine is going to be ruined either by inappropriate conditions, or, if marked correctly, by allowing inexpensive wines to age too long, and good wines not to age long enough.

■ Building your own wine cellar and then insulating and cooling and humidifying can be extremely rewarding. Personal touches and numerous creative ideas can add immensely to your pleasure of collecting and drinking wine. Such places are sanctuaries from the distractions and business of the day.

PART TEN

Vintage Chart

PART TEN

Vintage Chart

	CALIFORNIA		BURGUNDY		
	CABERNET	CHARDONNAY	RED	WHITE	RHONE
Outstanding Years	1990, 1991, 1992	1992, 1993			1978, 1989, 1990
Excellent Years	1970, 1974, 1976, 1978, 1984,1985, 1986, 1987, 1993	1990, 1991, 1984,1985, 1986	1971, 1978, 1985,1989 1990	1971, 1985, 1986, 1989, 1990, 1992, 1978	1970, 1979, 1983, 1985, 1988, 1991
Very Good Years	1973, 1975, 1977	1970, 1971, 1972,1973, 1975, 1978, 1979, 1980, 1981, 1982, 1983, 1988	1970, 1972, 1976,1987, 1988, 1992	1970, 1972, 1973, 1979, 1982, 1987, 1988, 1976, 1977	1972, 1980, 1981, 1982, 1986, 1987, 1993
Good Years	1979, 1980, 1981, 1982, 1989	1976, 1977,	1979, 1980, 1982,1986 1991, 1993	1980, 1981, 1983, 1991, 1993	1971, 1976, 1983, 1985, 1984, 1992
Average Years	1983, 1988	1974, 1987, 1989	1973, 1974 1975,1977, 1981, 1984	1984, 1974, 1975	1973, 1974, 1975, 1977
Below Average Years	1971, 1972				

	ITALY	SAUTERNES	BORDEAUX	GERMANY	DECLARED VINTAGE PORT
Outstanding Years	1985	1986, 1988, 1991	1982, 1983, 1986, 1989, 1990	1989, 1990	1977, 1983, 1985, 1992
Excellent Years	1971, 1974, 1978, 1988, 1991	1975, 1983, 1990	1970, 1971, 1979,1988, 1993	1971, 1976, 1983, 1985, 1988, 1991, 1992, 1993	1970, 1983, 1984, 1986, 1991
Very Good Years	1970, 1979, 1982, 1986, 1987, 1990	1970, 1971, 1976, 1980, 1985	1975, 1976, 1978, 1981, 1985, 1987	1975, 1979, 1981, 1982, 1986, 1987	1975
Good Years	1981, 1983, 1992, 1993, 1994	1978, 1979, 1982, 1987, 1992, 1993, 1994	1972, 1973, 1974,1977, 1980, 1984, 1991, 1992	1970, 1977, 1978, 1984	1972
Average Years	1975, 1976, 1973, 1977, 1980, 1984	1974, 1987, 1989	1973, 1974 1975,1977, 1981, 1984	1973, 1974, 1980	
Below Average Years				1972	

PART ELEVEN

Final Notes

Final Notes...

Wine, since it contains alcohol, is a controversial subject. For years, at least in the United States, it has been looked upon by some like all alcoholic beverages—as just another drug to obscure reality. Wine, however, offers much more. While no one can deny its ability to ease inhibitions, wine has a plethora of positive benefits. Besides its enhancing of food, and health and social benefits, wine lends a classy and thoughtful touch to many engagements and get togethers. It is an intelligent man's beverage. The warning labels that were plastered on the backs of bottles are an abomination to anyone who enjoys and understands wine; now, gladly that is about to change since the government is coming out with a new label more closely defining wine's place in our lives.

The government's proclivity for protecting us from ourselves with such warning labels is admirable—many countries wouldn't care what happened to its people. But while such warnings are noteworthy, some obscure and scare many from a beverage that may prove beneficial when used in moderation and with intelligence. Such is the case with wine. "Don't drink and drive" and other such admonitions are always a good reminder, but our perception of wine still has to change.

Moderate amounts everyday with meals is best—binge and episodic drinking on weekends is worst. Wine is a food; until both the government and its people learn to look at wine as a great product for our bodies, minds, and spirits, and treat it with the respect it deserves, it will continue to be either viewed as a harmful substance by the government, or abused by the people. It is up to all of us, then, to add to wine's prestige and place in society and government with our thoughtful consumption, and thoughtful and intelligent labeling from government. In the spirit of wine, let us all work together toward that goal.

Mike Lapmardo

A video tape will be available soon—call or write MC Productions.

About the Author...

Mike Lapmardo was born in 1952 and raised in Warren, Ohio. He is the oldest of five boys. Mike attended Warren J.F.K. High School and was active in athletics. He received a four year football scholarship to Thiel College in Greenville, Pennsylvania where he majored in English, Speech and Communications. Mike was the first recipient of the Ernest G. Heissenbuttel Award for outstanding achievement in the field of English Literature.

After his senior year in football, Mike was asked to try out for the Green Bay Packers, but after eleven years of organized football, he had had enough. Armed with his teaching certificate, Mike set out to do what he had always wanted to—teach. For fifteen years, Mike taught English and coached competitive speech and debate. His teams boasted over one hundred members each year, and were some of the most powerful and successful in the nation. In the 1987-1988 school year, they were not only state champs of Ohio, but came in first place in every local and national tournament they competed in.

In 1989, Mike teamed up with his brother, Chuck, a jet pilot and flight instructor and together they bought a wine store. In the next few years, Mike and Chuck—both educators in their own right—were now teaching people about wine. Their stores grew from one to four in number, and all boast tasting licenses where they can educate people right in the stores. The publication of this book, Mike says, is "the culmination of many dreams for both Chuck and me—and now hopefully we will be able to reach out to more people and teach them about something that is very special to us both—wine."

Mike enjoys skiing, gardening, occasionally building a house, drinking wine and vacationing in Carmel.